Sunsets After the Storms

Yvette Kilgore

Sunsets After the Storms

Copyright © 2022 by Yvette Kilgore

Published by Here I Am Publishing, LLC
780 Monterrosa Drive
Myrtle Beach, South Carolina 29572
www.hereiampublishingllc.com
info@hereiampublishingllc.com

Printed in the United States of America. This book is a work of non-fiction. Permissions have been obtained from those in the story. Jacket Photo Illustration licensed from Shutterstock Stock Photos (https://www.shutterstock.com).

Acknowledgement

I am acknowledging one very special person, Sandi Huddleston-Edwards, for providing everything that was necessary for me to write this book. Not only has she provided first, a beginning class on becoming an author, but countless hours of sharing her talent, her encouragement, and showing my ability to put into words what I want to share with others. In times of doubt, she encouraged me to write from my heart, and what I placed on paper could become a book I could be proud to share with others and use as a praise to God.

Along the way, we have become dear friends, and I will always be thankful for the friendship that continues to grow throughout our lives. I truly could not, and probably would not, have even attempted this step of writing words that has been on my mind and in my heart for so many years.

Sandi gives so much of her time and knowledge to others in such caring and loving ways and is truly a servant of God in her daily walk in this life. It has been a real blessing to have learned from her and to be able to call her my friend.

Thank you, my dear friend; you are loved.

Dedication

This book is dedicated to my family:

My husband, Gary, of fifty-five years.

My loving children, Lori, Jacob, and Jason.

My awesome grandchildren, Garrett, Liam, Jordan, Jonah, and Brayden.

Your love and encouragement have never been denied to me. Being a wife, mother, and Grammy to you have been my greatest achievements in life. I thank God for each of you every day.

"You are loved more than a bushel and a peck and a hug around the neck forever."

Love,
Yvette, Mom, Grammy

Table of Contents

"You'll Never Walk Alone"

When you walk through a storm
Keep your chin up high
And don't be afraid of the dark
At the end of the storm
Is a golden sky
And the sweet, silver song of a lark
Walk on through the wind
Walk on through the rain
Though your dreams be tossed and blown
Walk on, walk on with hope in your heart
And you'll never walk alone
You'll never walk alone
You'll never walk alone.

Prologue: Let's Get Married!

We were just kids when Gary and I decided we were all grown up. At nineteen-years-old and eighteen-years-old, respectively, we decided we should get married. *It will never last* is what everyone thought.

"They are too young. It's their first real relationship. They will be sorry one day."

I don't blame them for thinking these things. I would be thinking that today if one of my grandchildren at just eighteen or nineteen-years-old came and said, "Grammy, we are getting married!"

I could picture the future ahead for Gary and me. It was all good, of course. We would graduate from high school, get married, work, save money, buy our first little love shack, and start a family. It sounds easy, right? That was our plan. Our youth had it all figured out. However, there was just a slight change in those plans.

Our marriage would begin when Gary got home after finishing his training to be an Air Police Airman in the United States Air Force. After all his months of training were finished, he would then leave the U.S. to fly off to an overseas tour of duty, which would probably be in Vietnam where most new recruits were being sent during this time. We would have about a week together after our wedding; then I would stay with his mom and dad while he was gone.

There went my image of our little house with the white picket fence and a cute little golden cocker spaniel puppy (did I forget to mention her?) running around in the yard, while I picked my beautiful red tomatoes from the vine I would have planted. The actual events of our journey through the years are a little more complicated than that. It has been pretty entertaining in its own way with the ups and downs, some being humorous, some scary, and some sad and heartbreaking.

I'm going to share some of the events that occurred over many years, starting with our high school days in the '60s, when we were planning to marry during the time of the war in Vietnam and making difficult decisions, which included moves back and forth across the country, losing our home and all we had put into it, and health problems, which required organ transplants.

Many unexpected and unplanned things happen to all of us that we don't understand or like during life, and we find ourselves asking, "Why?" Life is hard, and there will always be challenges along the way. These hard times can defeat us, or we can seek ways to hang on and get through them no matter what they might be. We can find our way to good lives with hope instead of hopelessness. That is God's wish for all of us.

If my husband and I had not asked Jesus Christ to come into our lives, had not known God's love, and had not trusted and believed in His promises, our life together could have been a disaster. His promise gives us the assurance we can call on Him in our times of need. We know He will hear us and walk through it with us. He is our help during both the hard times and the good times. We have always tried not to let unknown or unwanted circumstances get us down to the point of living in fear and hopelessness, making our lives miserable and missing out on the joy and happiness God wants for us.

At times we have gotten sidetracked and allowed darkness to enter into our thinking. We have reacted to some things we didn't like only to make things worse for ourselves. Even so, God waited patiently until we turned back to Him, being faithful to His word. Then we could see His will being done. We continued to be thankful and strived to obey His teachings always, We wanted to be good examples for others, sharing the love He has for us, and we still do.

We quickly returned to the joy and happiness we knew and were able to live a life of goodness, not a life of misery and darkness. This is what I want for my children, my grandchildren, their children, and their children's children, and I want this for you, too, readers.

I am almost seventy-three years-old as I begin to write this book. My heart has been filled with hope and love for everyone, and I want to reach out and share the blessings and a special miracle God bestowed on my family's lives because we have chosen not to live in darkness and sin, which makes Satan happy, but we have made the decision to live in the light and love of Jesus Christ, Who makes it possible when we invite Him into our hearts.

So, come along with me as I recall our journey, starting in the late '60s. We had some funky dances back then. You might have heard of some of them but probably not all of them. I prefer to dance on this reminiscent journey, so if you are so inclined, come dance with me and enjoy the music and the memories I long to share.

CHAPTER 1: Our Beginning Path

*"The Lord will watch over your coming and
going both now and forevermore."*
--Psalm 121:8 (NIV)

Gary and I graduated from Taylor High School in North Bend, Ohio, in 1966. We grew up in the '50s and '60s during what I consider having been the best time to grow up. Life was easy then in the little towns where we lived, me in the small town of Cleves, Ohio, (not Cleveland) and Gary in North Bend, Ohio, the next town over as you make your way toward Cincinnati. North Bend is where the ninth President of the United States, William Henry Harrison, is buried. Gary and I didn't have to go far to see each other after we started dating. Actually, we could have walked to see each other; our towns were so close. Both towns are located near the bottom of Ohio in the southwest corner of the state along the Ohio River, bordering Indiana and Kentucky. We could be in either of the three states in about fifteen minutes from one to the other.

As teenagers in high school, we loved Friday night football games followed by sock-hops, dancing without our shoes on in the school gymnasium, so we would not ruin the basketball floor. Gary was on the football team, so I had fun cheering him on at each and every game. After the sock-hop, we would go across the border to Indiana, pull in to the A & W drive-in restaurant and order root beer floats that came in ice-cold frosted glass mugs. They were delivered on a tray that hung from the opened window of the car. They were so good. The frosted mug is what made them so special, I think.

The car was Gary's cool '59 Chevy Impala convertible. It was black with red interior and a black top, and we were stylin' big time. He got it when he was fifteen, and we loved making our rounds in it all over town. On other nights, we would be at one of the teen canteens around the area, dancing every dance we could until we were ready to drop. The dances back then were the greatest ever, along with being the best exercise anyone could do! There was, of course, the Twist and the Limbo that you probably have heard of, but there was also the Mashed Potato (always one of my favorites), the Locomotion, the Freddie, the Frug, the Hitch-Hike, the Shimmy, the Swim, the Watusi, the Bristol Stomp, the Boogaloo, the Jerk, the Monkey, the Strut, the Hully Gully, the Drag, the Pony, and, of course, the Funky Chicken. The Funky Chicken seems to have hung around forever, along with some others I'm sure I've forgotten about, too. We also really enjoyed a few of the great dances that started in the 1950s like the Stroll, the Jitterbug, and the Cha-Cha. We would make sure to dance to each and every song that was played -- as many times as we could during the night. We were just having good clean fun.

If you want to be entertained and have a laugh, search for the dances on the Internet unless you are familiar with them. They may seem pretty crazy to you compared to the dances of today, but we had the best time ever twisting our bodies, sliding our feet every which way, jerking, and jumping with all our energy. We were never bored; we just enjoyed being happy when we were dancing.

I feel a little bad for teens today, not having the same kind of safe dance places to go where they can just be kids and have good clean fun with everyone getting along without problems happening. We didn't have the type of peer pressure like there is today or drugs and guns all over the place with people shooting each other. We just wanted to have fun with everyone and enjoyed being young. What was even better, we found ways to be entertained and find enjoyment that did not require having a cell phone or video game to stare at or sit in front of all day long. We got out of the house and stayed active, and I know you are going to be really shocked when I tell you that we grew up with only one TV and only three TV channels to watch. But we never lacked being entertained by the shows that were on each night.

I know some of you are probably thinking, "Weren't there widespread race riots in the '60's. If so, how can she say it was a great time? I can say it because we grew up in small towns, we were all pretty much equal in every way, and we didn't want to fight like many people in the cities were doing. Of course, there were a few problems but nothing major like you read about whenever it gets violent. The majority in our towns respected each other and didn't have trouble getting along. I would be willing to say that if you talked to people who grew up in our little towns, they have nothing but great memories about growing up there. We went to school, had good clean fun, stayed out of trouble, and for the most part, did what we were told to do, and respected our elders. We were taught manners and right from wrong. Boy all that sure seems as if it got lost along the way -- especially respect!

"Love one another with brotherly affection.
Outdo one another in showing honor."
--Romans 12:10 (ESV)

CHAPTER 2: Learning a Good Work Ethic

"You shall eat the labor of your hands; you shall
be blessed, and it shall be
Blessed, and it shall be well with you."
--Psalm 128:2 (AMP)

My parents divorced when I was thirteen, leaving me certain there wouldn't be enough finances available for me to go to college. So, before I graduated from high school, I tested for positions with a few big companies in downtown Cincinnati. I accepted an offer for a job at the Cincinnati Bell Telephone Company, which it was called back then, to appear for work immediately after high school graduation.

I'd walk down to the bottom of the hill from our house and catch the bus to go to work. We rode all over the place before it finally got to my stop in Cincinnati. The fifteen-minute drive in a car took over an hour on the bus. There were never any problems riding back and forth, no matter where it stopped to pick up or dropoff other passengers. Cleves was actually at the end of the line for the bus from Cincinnati, so I saw each and every stop to and from town. By the time it got to Cleves, there was only a couple of us left on the bus before exiting.

I loved working at the phone company right from the start. The phone company was a great place to work with frequent raises and great benefits. I was excited, making my own money and opening a savings account to begin saving for my future wedding one day. Being in the city, window shopping at big department stores, and eating lunch in different places were all new and enjoyable to me.

I had dreamed of studying to become a commercial artist at college because I enjoyed sketching and drawing fashions and other items for newspaper and catalog advertisements. I spent all my spare time drawing people and fashions, pretending I was already working as an artist.

I still enjoy sketching and all types of art as a hobby, but it never became a career like I would have loved, but that is okay. Sometimes you just do what is needed in the circumstances you are in and the opportunities you have been given. Be thankful, as in my case, that you have a job. Make the best of it. The smartest thing to do in whatever job you are given is to give it your all and more, so you can be proud of yourself for a job-well-done.

I was rewarded for always doing the best I could in my jobs, whatever they might have been. While at the phone company, I earned a wonderful promotion within the first six months of employment. I was excited about the position because it was a one-person job. I was my own boss! I was in charge of what was called the Foreign Directory Department. It was fun to order telephone directories from all over the United States and some foreign countries, so companies were able to contact other businesses in different cities, states, and countries. This is when almost all communication was handled by writing letters and sending them in the snail mail or by making quick phone calls, not the long conference calls many companies make now. Instant communication with computers, texts, zoom, etc. wasn't available, so the phone directories were piled up in most companies' offices for information they relied on. It was interesting and fun to see all the different languages and types of information from each state and country. I could handle it all exactly as I wanted to, which was great. I was in charge of my own little domain; it was a pleasurable job for which I was getting paid well.

Before I left the company, I was offered another position as head of one of the biggest departments. I would have loved to accept the job, but by this time, I knew Gary and I would be getting married soon. I didn't think it was fair to accept the position for a short time, so I turned it down. I was thankful for the positions I held while working at the phone company. I learned valuable lessons about always doing my best and appreciating the opportunities I was given. These roles formed a good foundation for my work ethic in years to come. By doing a little extra than what was expected of me was noticed and led to other opportunities within the companies where I worked. It was always appreciated and led to many promotions throughout my years of working when we moved to different locations. Just give it your very best, with a little extra added for good measure.

The following is a great verse to consider and adhere to in all walks of life.

"The soul (appetite) of the lazy person craves and gets nothing [for lethargy overcomes ambition], but the soul (appetite) of the diligent [who works willingly] is rich and abundantly supplied."
--Proverbs 13:4 (AMP)

We should strive to live this way and pass it on to our children and grandchildren. Even when we might have to perform jobs we don't particularly like, we should still do them to the best of our abilities, no matter what it is. By doing this, it will make a more pleasant day for ourselves and those around us. We can feel good about ourselves at the end of each workday. Our actions and attitudes will be noticed and appreciated, leading to other open doors that can result in a job we will really appreciate one day. Be patient! Sometimes, we have to perform jobs we don't love; even so, learn to be thankful for each opportunity you are given along the way.

CHAPTER 3: Planning the Future / Regretful Decisions

"Husbands, in the same way be considerate as you live with your wives, and treat them with respect as the weaker partner and as heirs with you of the gracious gift of life, so that nothing will hinder your prayers."
--1 Peter 3:7 (NIV)

Attending college for an art degree would have been nice, but looking back, I believe one of our first blessings as a couple was the fact neither of us spent four years in college apart from each other. We probably wouldn't have gotten married to each other, and our lives wouldn't have turned out as it has.

God's plan is always the best plan! By the grace of God, we celebrated fifty-five years of marriage this year (2022). Out of curiosity, I searched to see if there was a special gift for the fifty-fifth year of marriage. Most countries had no traditional gift, but the flower suggested as a gift was a Calla Lily Plant! I found it interesting when the article claimed they are easy to grow in humid and moist areas, like the South where we live. After growing in a marriage for fifty-five years, it's nice to have suggested a plant that is really easy to grow, like a cactus! Just saying as we get older, we might forget to water the plants! Maybe better still, nice artificial flowers would be great for some of us!

After high school graduation Gary had first taken a job at the Seagram's Distillery in Lawrenceburg, Indiana, located right over the border from where we lived in Ohio. He worked there a short time before deciding to try a job with the railroad for a change. With my grandpa, uncle, and my dad all being railroad men, I guess he thought, "Why not?" He discovered it wasn't what he wanted to do. So, still not sure of what he wanted to do, he decided to enlist in the Air Force to serve the required four years of military duty.

Most young men were being drafted during this time and were being sent to serve in the war in Vietnam. Gary felt it would be best to enlist instead of waiting to be drafted. His brother-in-law had served in the Air Force, and Gary liked the idea of spending his tour of duty as an airman.

It was hard saying goodbye when Gary left for his training in San Antonio, Texas. We wrote lots of letters to each other and remained true to one another, planning the day when we would be married. Gary and I felt we were meant to spend our lives together, even if it meant we'd be apart while he was stationed overseas.

When Gary's basic training was finished, his parents and I went to visit him in San Antonio during his break before his technical training began. Because we thought his first assignment more than likely would be Vietnam, we decided we would get married before he left. Gary loves to get me going by telling everyone I asked him to marry me, but he forgets I have proof. My dad had framed the letter Gary wrote to him asking for my hand in marriage, as well as Dad's reply, giving him his consent. It is really special to me, not only because I can prove Gary asked me, and I did not ask him but because Dad kept it all those years. I have it to keep now.

I kept busy working, planning our wedding, and saving every bit of money possible to pay for our wedding, which would be simple and small. Including our parents and the wedding party, we'd have less than seventy-five attendees. We would have cake and punch in the church basement after the ceremony for all who attended the wedding. Later our family and wedding party would go to Gary's parents' house for a meal and to watch us open presents. Gary's father would grill some of his wonderful steaks with his special spice blend that made them so tender and delicious. That would be the extent of the reception. We'd have no band or dancing, just sharing a great meal together and opening presents. We would not have a honeymoon either. That would have to wait for another time, if ever.

Gary's mother and father were always so kind and thoughtful. They also offered a bedroom in their home for me to come and live after we got married and Gary would be leaving. I was so excited. It would be the first time in my whole life that I would have my own bedroom! They also would let me use one of their cars, so I could drive to work instead of taking the bus. I wouldn't have to get up as early to get to work on time. I'd be able to get some extra sleep each morning. I was happy with our plans. I didn't need a big wedding. And all was looking good so far.

I mentioned that my parents divorced when I was thirteen-years-old. The divorce had not been a friendly separation, and there were some harsh words being said about dad. Of course, I could understand the hurt Mom must have felt, but I didn't feel that she handled it well when speaking about him around us girls.

Divorce can cause so much hurt in many ways that others never recognize. We grew up in a time when most parents, and children didn't talk about their feelings, even when sensing that things were not right, and they were upset. It is so important to talk about feelings and emotions when things trouble you or when you don't understand what is happening within your family. I wish we would have discussed things when my parents decided to divorce. Absent of any real discussion, we would just clam up and go on like nothing was different for people to see. We just marched on bravely and smiled. That was a very harmful way of handling different situations that arose within our family. The only thing I can remember from it all was being confused and afraid of what else might happen to change things even more so in our house.

Experiencing work, marriage, separation, and divorce at a young age helped me to realize the reasons for so many problems between couples and children – a lack of conversation and openness. As Gary and I planned to be married, my hope was that we would have an open relationship with our future children. I hoped they would feel free to talk to us about anything that might concern them in the family and, most importantly, to always know their parents loved them. We would try our best to be there for them when they needed us in any way.

It is better to be open and truthful about what is going on and to explain why it is happening. This is the only way to build trust in others and help them learn what is right, what is wrong, and not to accuse others wrongly when not knowing the facts about what has happened. There are always two sides to every story.

"Whoever conceals his transgressions
Will not prosper, but he who confesses
And forsakes them will obtain mercy."
--Proverbs 28:13 (NIV)

Both of my parents remarried after a few years. Dad moved to Indianapolis, Indiana. My mom and her new husband bought a house in Miami Heights, Ohio, not far from Cleves. It was in the same school district, so I would be able to finish high school with my friends. The house was nice and very full! Besides Mom and her new husband, there was my maternal grandma, my sister, and me along with Mom's husbands' son and two daughters.

Now there were eight people living under one roof where before it had just been the three of us. Even though we had to share two bathrooms, we all got along just fine. Somehow, we all managed to be ready to leave when necessary for school or work. There were four bedrooms in the house. Grandma, my sister, and I shared a bedroom; the other two sisters shared a bedroom, and the son had his own bedroom, and then there was the master bedroom. There are some good memories of that time. It was just a big adjustment for all of us, and we made the best of it.

When Dad moved away, I had missed him. I always hung out with Daddy whenever I could before the divorce. I even ate sardines and avocados with French dressing poured on them whenever he was eating that so I could be near him and talk with him while we ate crazy things together. At least back when I was a kid, I thought they were crazy. I still am not a fan of sardines, but I do love avocados. Dad nicknamed me Gabby when I was little, not because I talked all the time, but because I loved an old cowboy hat I always wore when I was outside playing. I yanked it over my ears with the brim turned down. I was trying to look like the TV cowboy called *Gabby Hayes*, whom I loved to watch. I would pump my tricycle as fast as I could. After all, this was my version of a horse. In my mind, I was a real cowgirl.

Daddy's Girl! My dad and me.

Every single time anyone asked me what I wanted for my birthday or Christmas, my answer was always, "A horse!" There was no place to house one near our home, but I still asked for one. I miss hearing Dad calling me "Gabby,," but I have precious memories of him calling me that, which is priceless to me.

I would be the first to move out of the crowded house after Gary and I were married. But it would not change the number of girls living there for long. Mom gave birth to a beautiful baby girl, Amy, restoring the number to eight. Our wedding had been planned for June 30, 1967. Gary would be back from his training, and we were looking forward to that day.

Making decisions while planning a wedding with divorced parents was hard for me. I wasn't familiar with the proper way to word the invitation. Maybe I was too embarrassed to admit that and didn't want to ask for help. I had never really been to any wedding to see invitations and how they were worded in that situation, so I was on my own. I'm not sure of the reason, but I didn't think to just print Dad and Mom separately as the ones announcing the marriage of their daughter. I ended up using what was suggested, printing Mr. and Mrs. with Mom's new husband's name. It seemed the shortest way for it to be printed as I was trying to save money. The invitations hadn't seemed that important to me, but they were a disappointment after I received them and read what was printed.

I had tried to really stretch the one thousand dollars I had saved for all the expenses. My desire was to spend more on Gary's ring, my wedding gown, a small cake, and pretty flowers for the bouquets. I was so young and naïve. I didn't stop to think about who I was not mentioning on the invitations: my dad. That broke my heart knowing I had left him out. In my mind, I knew he was going to walk me down the aisle. I guess I took it for granted that everyone would know he was there for me. They all knew how important he was to me. After all, I was a Daddy's girl.

Unfortunately, there was no time to reprint the invitations. I felt terrible, and I never kept one for myself because of that. Dad never said a thing about it to me. He wouldn't have; Dad just wanted me to be happy. I was the one who had not been able to let go of that. My feelings were that I'd hurt him and had shown disrespect for my father.

"Love bears all things, believes all things,
Hopes all things, endures all things."
--1 Corinthians 13:7 (ESV)

CHAPTER 4: Assignment Blessings – 1967

"'For I know the plans I have for you,' declares
the Lord, 'plans to prosper you and not to harm
you, plans to give you hope and a future.'"
--Jeremiah 29:11 (NIV)

When Gary and hundreds of other airmen had finished their training, they were called to meet in a large auditorium for their graduation and to learn where they were being assigned for their first tour of duty. The officer in charge announced that he needed seven volunteers from the large group gathered there. Gary was a flight commander. He and his five squad leaders were sitting together with another flight commander on the other side of Gary.

Gary recalled his brother-in-law telling him, "Never volunteer for anything; it usually will be something you are not going to like, such as KP duty, being stuck in a kitchen all day, cooking and cleaning."

Regardless, Gary had a gut feeling, perhaps a little nudge from above, that he should volunteer. He told his five squad leaders he was going to volunteer, and they looked at him like he was crazy. The other guys who worked with Gary had grown to respect him, so when Gary stood up, they wanted to remain together, so they stood up, too. The other flight commander decided he'd volunteer and be the seventh. They didn't know what they were volunteering for, but they all did it together because Gary was led to stand and volunteer. Gary made a wise decision that day by paying attention to his gut feeling.

The seven men nervously waited to hear what they had just volunteered to do. The officer did not make them wait long.

He turned to them and said, "The seven of you are being assigned to duty at TUSLOG DET 30 in Ankara, Turkey." Then he turned to the other airmen in the auditorium and said, "The rest of you are going to do your tour of duty in Vietnam."

Out of the hundreds there, these seven men were blessed to escape the horrible assignment of going to Vietnam to fight in the war. Many of their friends and family had gone before them and had seen the horrors they could never have imagined facing. Many had lost their lives or returned home in pain and suffering in ways their lives would never be the same. History tells the heart-breaking story of this being a war that did not honor or show respect for all who fought there. They weren't given or shown any real thanks or recognition for risking their lives for others. There were no big celebrations when these soldiers returned home, no special honors displayed for them, and no homecoming parades organized for them as in previous wars when the soldiers returned at the end of a war. These soldiers were the forgotten Veterans who had fought and suffered and had seen the horrors of war, a war that had started in 1954 and did not end until 1975.

There are continued discussions as to whether it was a

blunder or a necessary war. It provoked anti-war protests and violence across the United States. There was so much death, destruction, and heartbreak for many families during that time and long after. Those with family members going into the military and Vietnam feared the worst for them. By God's grace, our family and the families of the other volunteers were spared from this fear and worry.

None of the seven had any idea where in the world Ankara, Turkey, was, but they knew they were not going to Vietnam. That was a reason for praise and thanksgiving.

The promise in Psalms 121 (NIV), which tells us God is always with us, was shown to be true for Gary that day.

A song of ascents.
"I lift up my eyes to the mountains—
where does my help come from?
My help comes from the LORD,
the Maker of heaven and earth.
He will not let your foot slip—
he who watches over you will not slumber;
indeed, he who watches over Israel
will neither slumber nor sleep.
The LORD watches over you—
the LORD is your shade at your right hand
the sun will not harm you by day,
nor the moon by night.
The LORD will keep you from all harm—
he will watch over your life;
the LORD will watch over your coming and
going both now and forevermore."

That was just the beginning of the proof and assurance for us that God's promise is real. He was and would be with us every step we took in our lives because we both chose to believe in Jesus and asked Him into our hearts. Some of the times I will share with you have humor in them, so you will chuckle. There are others that involve very unusual events that no one had expected. Also, as life goes, some tell of pain and sadness. These things are part of everyone's lives while living on this earth. There will be many different circumstances taking place all through our journey.

You will probably be able to relate to some of our family experiences as you read about them. I pray you will also be able to realize that good sometimes comes from things that are considered devastating or heart-breaking while going through them, making you feel hopeless and lost. But most of the time, when you reflect back, you can see how some of those hard times led to a path that resulted in wonderful and special moments that may not have happened otherwise.

We alone choose to live in ways that control our outlooks and attitudes toward the trials we face and how they will affect us. We have two choices in deciding that. One will cause us to feel hopeless and defeated; the other choice will give us hope and joy so we can continue on with our lives without getting discouraged. My prayer is that by sharing these events from my family's lives, you will be encouraged to search for and receive the way to make the choice that will assure hope and happiness through your journey in life.

"When anxiety was great within me,
Your consolation brought me joy."
--Psalm 94:19 (NIV)

CHAPTER 5: From a Wedding to Overseas

"Do not be yoked together with unbelievers.
For what do righteousness and wickedness
have in common? Or what fellowship can light
have with darkness?"
--*2 Corinthians 6:14* *(NIV)*

The year was 1967. I attended Cleves United Methodist Church that was situated on a hill. This church was located right down the street from a little house where Gary had been born. Who knew the many times when I'd gone past that house on Sundays as I traveled to church that I would one day marry the boy who had been born there on June 25, 1948? And he'd been born just three months before I was born in September of 1948.

The minister of my church had been reappointed to a different area to meet the needs of a church there. The moving of Methodist ministers happened frequently in those years. He would be gone before our wedding occurred, and the new minister would not be there in time to officiate. So, we had some decisions to make.

I loved my little church, which had the most beautiful stained-glass window behind the altar. I wanted that window in our wedding pictures. Even though most of the pictures would be in black and white, I planned to get at least one of Gary and me and the wedding party in color. Gary and his family were fine with us being married at my church. The location was more central for family and friends who would be attending. Gary's parents' house was also closer to this church for the family and friends who were invited to the reception meal.

Gary and his parents attended a Baptist church, which was located in another town near Cincinnati. We asked Gary's pastor if he would come to my church and perform the wedding ceremony for us. I had attended church with Gary and his family in the past and had met the pastor, so he already knew me. He and Gary's dad had become good friends, so we were pretty confident he would do that for us. He immediately agreed and we found it amusing we were going to be married in a Methodist Church by a Baptist minister. It was exciting to include both of our families' churches this way.

So, on June 30, 1967, just five days after Gary turned 19-years-old, we were married in the little white church on top of the hill with the beautiful stained glass window's vibrant colors shining brightly through to the altar. Dad, who was sobbing like a baby, walked his eighteen-year-old baby girl down the aisle to the altar where her high school sweetheart stood waiting for her to become his wife. I had been tempted to wear my old cowboy hat down the aisle, but that would have made Dad cry even more. He had a hard time as it was. When the minister asked, "Who gives this woman to be married to this man?" Dad could hardly speak.

The little church was cheerful; my simple lace sheath dress with the long tulle veil was just what I had wanted; my bridesmaid's dresses were a soft shade of light peach; and my bridesmaids were beautiful as they carried their colorful bouquets. Everything appeared perfect to me. Gary looked handsome in his white jacket and black pants with his groomsmen standing by him.

Gary and I recited our vows in the presence of God and received His blessing for our union as man and wife. We were so excited and happy for more than just being married to one another. We had another blessing we were celebrating also. Before Gary came home for our wedding, he had learned the tour to Ankara, Turkey, now allowed spouses to join their husbands or wives. I'd be able to live in Turkey with him. We had never even dreamed of being together until after his tour of duty was over. This was a blessing we hadn't considered possible. God's plan for us is always better than we can imagine when we put our trust in Him.

> *"Now the God of perseverance and*
> *encouragement gives you all the same*
> *purpose, following the example of Christ*
> *Jesus, so that you may together give glory*
> *to the God and Father of our Lord Jesus*
> *Christ with one heart."*
> *–Romans 15:5-6 (AMP)*

This is the little white Methodist Church
I attended and where Gary and I were
married.

Our wedding picture -- after our vows
were recited in the presence of God.

Our parents were with us on this
special day. Left to right, my parents,
me, Gary, and Gary's parents.

CHAPTER 6: Welcome to Turkey

"Her husband is respected at the city gate,
where he takes his seat among the
elders of the land."
--Proverbs 31:23 (NIV)

I wouldn't be able to travel to Turkey with Gary, but I would be going instead of us being apart for years. Tons of necessary paperwork was required after he arrived in Turkey, as well as required paperwork for me to complete. Then both sets would be reviewed before allowing me to join my husband. I'd need to have a physical examination and the necessary inoculations to enter Turkey. Obviously, it would be a few months before approval was granted. This allowed time for me to take the Civil Service Test and get a GS rating, which would enable me to work for the Air Force in some capacity while living in Turkey.

Along with the background checks and assurance I wasn't an anti-war protester, we had to provide proof we'd be able to pay rent and the other bills while living together. There wasn't an actual Air Force Base in Ankara with housing for married couples like in many other countries. We'd be living in the city among Turkish citizens. Finally, the last of the red tape was proof that if I had to return to the U.S. quickly, my family or Gary's family could afford my travel expenses and not be a hardship on the Air Force.

Most of the single and married guys (whose wives hadn't joined them), bunked together in the Airmen's Billets, in a building where Gary's Unit, TUSLOG DET 30, was located. This building housed the mess hall and the Air Police headquarters. Gary, an Air Police Airman, lived in the Billets until he'd rented our apartment before I'd arrive. Ah yes, the apartment that awaited my arrival. The events in store for me have to be described in a way that imagery will help you understand what my first night in a foreign country was like – all because I wanted to be with my new husband.

I was the only passenger on the plane by the time it landed in Ankara, Turkey. The other passengers had departed at one of the stops scheduled on this flight from New York. There weren't as many travelers crossing the ocean in the '60s like today, so direct flights were not common. Flying across the pond usually entailed more stops on the same flight.

I arrived in Turkey at a very late hour. It was pitch black at the airport when we landed. Not just the sky, but all the surrounding area as far as I could see was nothing but darkness. As I walked down the steps of the airplane and got to the bottom step, I looked around. There wasn't anything else to do but keep walking toward the little airport building. It looked scary to me because all I saw were Turkish men standing guard around the building; not one US Air Force personnel was in sight.

The door to the airplane was closed, and it was preparing for departure. It wouldn't be sticking around; they were in the air before I could climb back up into the plane. I was frightened, imagining something was wrong. Maybe the plane had been forced to land in a different airport. Maybe they had taken me to the wrong place. How would I ever get out of here if I couldn't communicate with anyone?

Few people were inside the building along with little ol' me with blonde hair and looking lost. Not only were there only Turkish men, but they had very dark hair. I stood out like a flying fish being a blonde. I felt like all eyes were focused on me; this I didn't like. I tried to force back the tears; hoping no one noticed my fear of being alone in the middle of nowhere. I was unable to speak. That's when I noticed men's shoes descending the stairs from a second floor. Relief! The man wearing those shoes wore a United States Air Force uniform. I was being rescued! It wasn't Gary, but I was just so relieved to see someone who would understand me and to have someone I could talk to about my situation. He looked my way and smiled and waved as he walked toward me.

> *"So do not fear, for I am with you; do not be dismayed, for I am your God. I will strengthen you and help you."*
> *--Isaiah 43:10 (NIV)*

After introducing himself, he explained Gary was waiting upstairs in an unrestricted area and didn't yet have clearance rights for this restricted area. He apologized it wasn't Gary who had come to greet me. Finally, I began breathing normally again and thanked God for my safety. Admittedly, I was close to having what I imagined to be a panic attack.

Unfortunately, there was unrest between Turkey and the United States at this time because of events happening between Turkey, Cyprus, Lebanon, and Greece, to name a few. Even though troops had been sent there to aid the situation, some of the Turkish people were unhappy about Americans being in their country and made it well-known.

The things I'd heard about Turkey had me on edge: don't be overdramatic, be careful, don't argue with the Turkish people, and never insult their country, customs, or anything Turkish. We were seen as guests in their country. If any problem arose and we were around, it would be considered our fault. We would be arrested, charged with a crime, and sent to prison. We would be the only guilty party – no matter what. Their reasoning was if we'd not been there, the problem wouldn't have happened. I was determined to watch my "Ps" and "Qs" and keep my mouth shut. I would keep my distance from any situation that might go wrong and seen as if I'd instigated it.

I found that being in any foreign country with different cultures, laws, and languages was difficult, but it was necessary to show respect and learn. After all, we were living among the Turkish citizens and their authorities instead of a U.S. Air Force Base under their protection. Of course, I knew this would be different from the town of Cleves, but I wasn't prepared for carefully choosing my words constantly. Not one to make trouble, I might say something incorrectly or make an issue if they took offense to something I might have done.

Whenever they were expressing their dislike for Americans, I quickly learned not to argue or try to retaliate in any way. It was hard because we were spat on and had small rocks thrown at us while we were quietly walking from one place to another. We walked almost everywhere we went, so we were out in the city most days with the Turkish citizens. Thankfully, we were never seriously injured. It took a lot of discipline to remain quiet when they were yelling, "Get out of Turkey. We don't want you here.!"

I struggled not to point out that we were there as a member of JUSMAT (Joint US Military Aid Turkey). We kept our mouths shut and walked away.

I found it worrisome I might make a general statement about something Turkish that wouldn't come out correctly and would be perceived as a criticism or starting a problem that would conclude with a call to the police. Thankfully, Dad's nickname for me, Gabby, wasn't because I never kept my mouth shut. There could have been big trouble if I portrayed the name. As with any country, even our own, different circumstances require you to make the best of a situation.

The initial Turkish Penal Code stated that anyone who publicly denigrated "Turkishness" would be punished by imprisonment of between six months to two years. Now it states "Turkish Nation" (Turkish Penal Code) as of April 30, 2008.

The reasons for some of these punishments seem harsh but may be ones the United States may want to consider enforcing: burning the flag; displayed disrespect and hatred toward the president of the United States, military, and the police. It's strictly my opinion, but there's just too much hatred in the world today – more than I've ever experienced.

Of course, not all Turkish people hated us, just certain groups, like those all over the world today that cause problems. All countries have good people and evil people. Too many have forgotten about respect and care for their brothers and sisters of the world. The devil is really wreaking havoc.

But I digress. Allow me to return to my arrival in Turkey and the apartment I entered that dark night.

CHAPTER 7: Home Away from Home

"The foreigner residing among you must be
treated as your native-born. Love them as
yourself, for you were foreigners in Egypt. I
am the LORD your God."
--Leviticus 19:34 (NIV)

After getting my luggage and climbing the steps, I was finally with Gary. I melted in his arms, happy and relieved to finally be with him. I never wanted to let go. Shortly, we piled into the car and drove to Ankara. At night, it seemed like a long drive. In the daylight, it didn't seem quite as long. But it was so dark that night I thought we'd never see lights again.

Finally, after forever, we were in Ankara. Most newly married couples start out madly in love. They long to do all they can to make the other happy. They don't argue much in the beginning. Everything is saturated in love. Everything is brighter. But not quite so yet, I was about to discover. Gary had waited to tell me he'd only have time to get me and my luggage into our apartment before he'd have to report back to duty. They had been on alert of a potential crisis, so he and the Air Police were on duty, no exceptions. When duty called, you were there.

Our building appeared old and dark. As we walked toward it, I searched for an entrance door, possibly a lobby, and some light. I didn't see anything except a set of stairs off the sidewalk, which descended to the lower level of the building. I assumed we'd find the elevator and go up to our apartment behind that door, but instead, when Gary opened the door, I realized that this was not where we would get on an elevator, but in fact, this was the door into our apartment, a basement apartment.

We entered the apartment with me trying to process that Gary wasn't going to stay as he had to return to duty. Vaguely, I heard him say, "You must be tired after that long flight. You should get ready for bed and get some rest." He gave me a quick kiss, opened the door, and said something about trying to return sometime tomorrow before I could say a word. This had seemed insane so far and nothing like how I'd pictured our first night together here. And this apartment wasn't making me feel any better.

I wandered around the little space and found the kitchen. It was like a closet with a little counter, a small sink with running water (which I was told not to drink), a hot plate with one burner, and no refrigerator of any kind – not even the mini under-the-counter kind. I had all the comforts of home to enjoy while I sat and watched a movie while waiting for him to return. NOT!

I was spooking myself and afraid to sit on the sofa, which was pretty rough looking. But it didn't matter. There wasn't anything to do in the living room anyway – no television, no radio, no record player, and no telephone. It was too bad cell phones weren't being used yet. If so, I could have called Gary for reassurance. But I had no way to communicate with him or anyone for that matter. I was definitely isolated and alone. The only thing to do was to stay in the dark basement apartment and hope that he would be able to return tomorrow.

Everything was dark and seemed to grow even darker. Small rectangular windows with little curtains on either side looked out onto the street. Of course, they were dark and dreary looking. I had nothing to occupy my mind and put me at ease, help me to relax, and make me feel comfortable. Gary had been thoughtful enough to have snacks and bottled water sitting on the counter in the kitchen if I were starving, but I really didn't think I could eat a thing.

I did notice a big, galvanized garbage can sitting on the floor in the so-called kitchen and could not figure out why we would need such a big one like that. Nothing else had magically appeared to make this space really look like a functioning kitchen. But apparently, we would be having lots of trash to throw away and a big garbage can to put it all in.

Next, I went into the bedroom to take a peek. There was a low bed that my luggage was lying on. It didn't look comfortable at all. I failed to check if it was sitting on concrete blocks or something. I knew I wasn't going to be climbing into my jammies and cuddling down in that bed for a restful night's sleep. When I glanced into the little bathroom, my eyes fixed on an odd-looking toilet with a wooden box above it on the wall and a hanging chain, which I assumed was how you flushed it. A tiny shower and an even tinier sink were not exciting to me either.

Finally, I returned to the low bed and sat beside my luggage. I listened to the silence until every so often, I would see feet walking past the windows and hear a man loudly calling, what sounded like, "Eskagee. Eskagee. Ollie. Ollie. Es-kagee." My mind played tricks on me as I imagined all kinds of things those words might mean. It would be a very long night, without the possibility of sleep. My ears were on high alert. I thought, *If someone tries to get in the door, well, I guess I can throw the big garbage can at them!*

I listened for hours, not knowing what to expect but still trying to imagine what they could be yelling about all though the night. Finally, I decided if there was trouble, someone would have reported it, and the police would have come by now. I figured, if no one else in this building is worried about it, I might as well quit making myself so scared and calm down. At least I did accomplish that, knowing I wasn't going to fall to sleep.

"Fear of man will prove to be a snare,
But whoever trusts in the Lord is kept safe."
--Proverbs 29:25 (NIV)

I didn't unpack my suitcases, nor did I change my clothes. Instead, I just sat on the edge of the horrible bed and waited, praying the morning light would come soon. Then I could peek out the window to see what things looked like on the street, or at least I could see what kind of shoes people wore – anticipating that would be interesting.

I thought at least I'd have something interesting to write home about: describing my first night in Turkey. It would be nothing they could have expected to hear from me or even imagined. This would give me something to do while I waited for Gary to finally return from duty, whenever that might be. Fortunately, I'd packed stationery, so I could spend time writing letters. The note home might have started out something like this.

Hi everyone,

Let me tell you about my first night in Turkey. It was a DARK night, and I was in the DARK basement apartment all alone watching feet go by the little windows with DARK curtains hanging on each side of them. A man started yelling some crazy sounding gibberish all night long that I did not understand that sounded like "Eskagee, Eskagee, Ollie Ollie Eskagee." Also, I could not find anything that resembled a refrigerator anywhere in the place. I just sat on the uncomfortable bed, awake all night, waiting and waiting for Gary. He had not been able to stay with me; he had to report right back to work after he brought me here from the airport. Really wish you were all here.

"I have set the Lord always before me, because
he is at my right hand, I shall not be shaken."
--Psalm 16:8 (ESV)

CHAPTER 8: From Darkness to Light

"Cast your cares on the Lord, and He will
sustain you; He will never let the righteous
be shaken."
--Psalm 55:22 (NIV)

Gary finally returned the next day. I must have looked a fright from not sleeping. He tried to assure me things would be better. All I could do was trust him and hope he could at least stay the night, not having to leave me alone two nights in a row after just arriving with nothing to do and not having a good meal in a while.

When I asked about the kitchen and the big garbage can, his answer wasn't encouraging at all. He explained we'd get ice and put it in the garbage can. We'd be able to keep food cool then. This was about the time I began thinking, *I wonder if I can get a ticket back to the United States easily?*

He must have seen the doubt on my face and knew he'd better let me know his plans. He explained this apartment was the only thing he could get for my first couple of nights here. It was close enough for him to walk to and from work, when necessary, because of the high alert situation. He didn't want my travel plans to change because it would have meant more paperwork to complete and delayed my coming. There was no way of anticipating a potential problem would happen when it did, which occurred after I was in the air and on my way to Turkey. Gary just kept repeating how sorry he was about how everything had turned out for my first night here.

Gary told me about the plans he'd arranged that would take place soon. I finally had something to look forward to, lifting my doubts about coming to Turkey to be with him. I never confessed I'd considered returning to the states after this first night's experience without him here. He assured me we would be together that night and the next day and night. I wouldn't be alone. More good news was that in a couple of days, a better apartment would be available in a nice building where other American military couples lived. Gary had already made the arrangements for us to move into it. From then on, when he did have to work nights, I would have other Americans around me I could talk to.

"Everyone watches out for each other if they happen to need anything. Also, there is a night guard on duty in the entrance of the building, so we'll be very safe living there. No one will try to start a problem."

Thank the Good Lord in Heaven! This apartment wasn't going to be our home the entire time we lived in Turkey. I could have shouted to the top of my lungs, "Hallelujah! Praise God!" But then, I was afraid of getting into trouble.

Indeed, Gary stayed with me and was there until it was time for us to move to the new apartment. We chose to leave the old apartment by slipping away in the night to avoid any problems or arguments with the landlord. Gary had paid the full month's rent that had been agreed upon. So, we were not cheating him out of any money. But with things so different here, we didn't want to have any other kind of fee to pay. We figured the landlord would be ahead anyway by us only having been there a few days after paying for a whole month. Besides, we left the nice big galvanized garbage can there, too, so I figured they came out way ahead!

We just gathered up my luggage, which I'd never fully unpacked and made our way up the hill toward our new place. I practically ran because I was so anxious to arrive at the new apartment. The farther we climbed the hill, I noticed the buildings were looking better and brighter, filled with light. They seemed newer and better-built structures.

It wasn't too long before he stopped in front of a very nice apartment building and said, "This is it!"

We entered the building through a nice door into an entrance that was lit up and had nice clean floors. The night guard was on duty and greeted us. I was happy to see we were going up the steps to our new apartment. There would be no more looking at feet walking by. There were no elevators, but this was just a three-story building, so it didn't really matter. On the second floor is where he unlocked and opened the door. Gary turned on lots of lights as we entered our new apartment. This is where we'd be living during our time in Ankara. I couldn't believe my eyes as I looked around.

The apartment was bright and cheerful with huge windows across the back that looked out over the back yard with a pool. Granted it was a small cement pool and the water was a shade of green, but Gary quickly told me there were medics living in the building.

"They are always testing the water to ensure it is safe for us to swim. We won't get sick. The water just turned green.

Think of it as a lake!"

It was all good. We spent many days in that pool and were thrilled to have it right in our back yard. Later, after we were back in the states, we received a letter from friends still there with an enclosed picture, showing the pool had collapsed because of an earthquake that had happened close by. This was sad for us because we remembered all the fun times we'd had, and now others who would move in wouldn't have the pool to enjoy.

Next, we looked around at our big living room area with a balcony off the back and furniture that was clean, sturdy, and comfortable-looking. On one wall was an alabaster fireplace that was beautiful! I had never heard of alabaster until I got there.

Next to the living room was a big dining room that looked out over the back yard. This dining room window was the one I stood at one morning when after I had opened the curtains to let the sunlight in, I was shocked to see sheep were being slaughtered in the back yard. I wanted to turn away, but my attention was held as I watched the sheep submit to this act. The sheep would have their necks rubbed, become very relaxed, look peaceful and then suddenly have their throats slit. Then they were slaughtered. It was such a horrible sight, but watching the sheep wait instead of running away and walking up to be the next one to have the same fate was something that was reminding me of a Biblical teaching in the book of Isaiah. It told of Jesus' obedience.

"He was oppressed and afflicted, yet he did not
open his mouth; he was led like a lamb to the
slaughter, and as a sheep before its shearers, is
silent, so he did not open his mouth."
--Isaiah 53:7 (NIV)

I discovered this was a holiday called Kurban Bayrami (The Feast of the Sacrifice), which is one of the oldest Islamic holidays in Turkey. The meat from the sheep is shared with visiting relatives and neighbors and given to the poor. It made me feel better, knowing it was all for a very good reason.

Let's go back to looking around the new apartment the first night there. Gary then showed me not one but two bedrooms and a very nice bathroom that was all white tile from floor to ceiling. There was even a ringer-washing-machine in there. I would not have to haul clothes to wash them somewhere, which was a real bonus. Gary explained the extra bedroom was where everyone put up lines to hang clothes inside to dry. You didn't want to hang them outside because all the-soot from the coal they burned around the city would make the clothes black. To prove this, each day, my blonde hair had black specks in it from walking around outside. So, it was great to be able to dry our clothes inside where it was soot free.

I did realize though, that I would be doing a lot of ironing from this point in time by not having a dryer. But when you are a newlywed, you do what you need to do so your hubby will be happy and his uniforms will look just right. I spent many years starching and ironing his shirts when he wore his dress blues and also his khaki uniforms for daily duties. These were not fun trying to make sure they were creased perfectly and wrinkle free. I do hope all the servicemen get their khakis done for them these days, so their spouses do not have to spend hours getting them to look perfect.

Next, he took me into the most exciting part of the apartment for me: It was a real honest to goodness kitchen. There was not a hot plate or a tin can full of ice. This kitchen was one where we could store food in a nice refrigerator, and it had a freezer, too! I would be cooking on a gas stove with an oven, not on a hot plate. What a great feeling, knowing we would not be taking food out of a garbage can to eat! I was absolutely ecstatic.

There also was a big double sink and a built-in draining board in the counter, along with lots of counter space to work on. A real plus for me was that there was a door in the kitchen that went out to a little balcony on the side of the apartment. I loved that I could have fresh air when I was cooking. If I burned anything, I could quickly toss it out the door, and when Gary got home, he would never know I ruined dinner!

I had not cooked a lot, so this was all going to be a learning experience with me making edible meals to feed Gary. I could make breakfast okay, but I had not really shopped for lots of ingredients to make full meals. I was used to Mom, Grandma, or Gary's Mom doing all the cooking of dinners before I had arrived in Turkey. Thank goodness I had packed my *Betty Crocker Cookbook* that we had received as a wedding gift and brought it along with me, so I was ready, willing, and able. Betty Crocker taught me to cook many meals while I was over there.

Gary was easy to please with meals. If there was hamburger in whatever I made, he was happy. I learned to mix up a mean meatloaf, which made him really happy. It is still one of his favorite meals after all these years: meatloaf and mashed potatoes any day would be just fine with him. I became sick of meatloaf, so he usually only gets it when he orders it out in restaurants now.

Things were definitely looking up and continued to get better and better from that point on. The new apartment was like a mansion to us after that basement apartment. We were very happy and very comfortable. We were being watched over, and all was good. Thanks be to God. We made many close friends that lived in the same building and others when we attended the church services held every Sunday with the Chaplain in the Billets. Some of those friends are still in touch with us today, which is great. We have been able to share pictures and stories about our children and grandchildren. We feel like we are still connected.

Soon, after we were settled in our new apartment, I got a position working for the Air Force in the USO office. It was a good way to spend my day and earn extra spending money. I enjoyed helping to bring entertainment over for everyone to enjoy.

Things were falling into place for Gary and me. We were being a grown up, responsible married couple making our way in Turkey. We were enjoying every moment of living and learning about another part of the world. We considered it a great education in many ways and felt we had a head start on life by being able to experience this while we were so young.

"Each of you must take responsibility for doing the creative best you can with your own life. Be very sure now, you who have been trained to a self-sufficient maturity, that you enter into a generous common life with those who have trained you, sharing all the good things that you have and experience."
--Galatians 6:5-6 (MSG)

CHAPTER 9: A Different Way of Living

"Therefore, I urge you brothers and sisters,
in view of God's mercy, to offer your bodies
as a living sacrifice, holy and pleasing to God
-- this is your true and proper worship. Do
not conform to the pattern of this world but
be transformed by the renewing of your mind.
Then you will be able to test and approve what
God's will is -- his good, pleasing,
and perfect will."
– Romans 12:1-2 (NIV)

Because there wasn't a military base in Ankara, the different departments of the military branches were located in many scattered buildings around the city. Some were close enough for us to walk to, but when we needed to go to Balgat or other places farther away to shop, we had to take a taxi.

Balgat was just outside the city of Ankara where one building contained the commissary, and a few other buildings were used for different military departments. The commissary (a military supermarket) was where we went for most of our shopping—almost like shopping in America. We were able to get all the things needed for groceries and other items like we were used to getting in the United States because of shipments from America.

We learned where to get a reliable taxi driver who would take good care of us. We didn't want to worry about being taken the long route, so our fare would be more. We also relied on the drivers not to take us into trouble spots where we might be in danger of an anti-American protest or riot. The trusted taxi drivers would stop and turn around if they saw something like that ahead. While it didn't happen often, we appreciated our drivers for not continuing when they noticed something wrong. There was an instance where a couple couldn't get turned around, so the taxi driver told the couple to get out of the vehicle and begin running away as fast as they could before the police came. Thank God for the drivers who cared and kept us from danger.

There were times when we shopped in the city for Turkish items. There were beautiful antelope leather jackets and coats and cute women's shoes. We purchased gifts for everyone back home: beautiful alabaster or brass items, Turkish towels, and jewelry, among other things. The rings we purchased for our family and ourselves were gorgeous. I still have mine and treasure them.

What I especially loved when shopping in the Turkish shops was the bargaining. Back and forth negotiating until a price was reached – what we could afford to pay or what we'd decided we wanted to pay. After all, money was needed for other things, too. Very few customers paid the asking prices. The shop owners didn't want you to leave empty-handed, so they ensured you got the price you wanted to pay so you would not go to another shop and purchase the same item at a better price. The bargaining was a fun part about living in Turkey.

When we visited the country in 2012, I couldn't resist

buying two more rings when shopping at the Grand Bazaar in Istanbul. In was fun to be able to bargain once again to get the prices we wanted to pay.

Prices at the Balgat commissary couldn't be bargained. They were priced very well, much lower than prices in America for the same items. Military life had good benefits and was a great life when war wasn't involved. I wouldn't have minded being a military wife for another twenty years or more if things had been different. After living in Turkey during the '60s, my shopping ways in America had to be reset when I first returned back home because I wanted to bargain with the salespeople for items to purchase. Of course, that didn't work in America!

Fruits and vegetables could be bought from the Turkish economy, but we only purchased our meats from the commissary. The Turkish butchers usually did not refrigerate the meat they sold. In fact, you would see whole skinned lambs, chickens, and other meat hanging in the butcher shop window with the hot sun beating through. This wasn't very appetizing, let alone not being safe to eat. In the '60s, Ankara's practices were behind, while Istanbul was a more modern city, and located on the European side of the country, whereas Ankara was on the Asian side. We were careful where we shopped for any kind of food. We did, however, buy bread that was sold out of the back of a pickup truck, especially if we timed it right, and the bread was still warm. That was the best way to get it.

We learned to like lamb, particularly the Turkish lamb, Döner Kebabs. They were delicious. We found the best place to go and sit down to eat them without worrying about getting sick from eating there. It became a once-a-week outing. I've not eaten one as good as those, my mouth still waters whenever I think of the tender and juicy lamb sliced thin and piled on the pita. Delicious!

Then there were times when we'd purchase our needs from the city's black market stores. Many of the shipments from America would be illegally obtained and sold on the Turkish economy. We refrained from doing this often, but the Black-Market stores seemed to always have things the commissary didn't have in stock. Of course, we paid much more for the items than at the commissary, which kept this from being a habit. Black-markets was a new concept and life lesson as we didn't shop at these stores in our small town of Cleves, Ohio. Maybe there were some in the bigger cities around us, but I wasn't aware of them.

As usual, not all Turkish people performed illegal acts or hated Americans. We met some wonderful Turkish citizens who treated us well. The owner of our building was a former Turkish military officer. He lived in the building, actually the floor above us – the top floor. This man was really good to Gary and me. He even took us to see the famous basketball team, the Harlem Globe Trotters, when they were in Ankara, playing against the Turkish basketball team. We'd never seen the Globe Trotters in person before, so this was a real treat for us. Meadowlark Lemon was on the team and the best at trick shots. He put on a real show of his talents. During their trip to Ankara, the Globe Trotters visited the airmen at the billets and had breakfast with them to show their appreciation for their duty in Ankara.

If you are too young to have seen or heard of Meadowlark Lemon, go online and watch videos of him in his prime. He was a great man in many ways. Gary had the honor of being invited to a Turkish man's home. He was one of the Turkish men who worked at the billets to keep all the airmen's dress shoes spit-shined and looking perfect. He took Gary to his village outside of Ankara to meet and eat a meal with his family. Gary found it very special to have been invited into their modest home. He was touched by the invitation and has never forgotten the experience.

We invited this friendly and caring man into our home several times, always enjoying his company. He appreciated being hired to shine the airmen's shoes. Unfortunately, he wasn't able to bring his family to visit us, which I regretted. It would have been nice to know them, too.

Gary and the man became close friends. Whenever I think of what he said to Gary, I get tears in my eyes. As Gary was getting ready to leave when his tour of duty was over in Ankara, he and Gary were thanking each other for all the good times they had shared and saying their goodbyes.

"We were both getting a little sad," Gary said, "realizing we'd probably never see each other again. He got a little choked up and said to me, 'You know my friend. Lots of airmen come and go over the years, and there are always good ones and bad ones. Sometimes, really bad and really good. My friend, you are one of the really good ones, and I will miss you very much.'"

The message from his statement is universal: treat each other with kindness, show love for one another, and you will be treated with kindness and loved in return. Gary's tour of duty in Ankara, Turkey, was in God's plan for him. God's love had been silently spoken, so Gary would know to stand and volunteer that day in Texas. Gary and six others out of the hundreds were blessed not to go to war in Vietnam. And I was to join in Gary's blessing by being with him in Ankara, Turkey, as we were beginning our life together as man and wife.

Earlier, I shared stories about being scared when I first arrived in Turkey and the different things that weren't pleasant, but I was there and Gary was there. Nothing that happened around us could even compare a tiny bit to what the other men who were sent to Vietnam had to experience and endure. We suffered nothing compared to the fear and worry their loved ones withstood. To this day I give thanks for the blessing we were given in 1967 when Gary felt the nudge, instructing him to volunteer.

"For the sake of Christ, then, I am content with weaknesses, insults, hardships, persecutions, and calamities. For when I am weak, then I am strong."
--2 Corinthians 12:10 (NIV)

CHAPTER 10: Experiences of a Lifetime

*"The LORD shall preserve thy going out and
thy coming in from this time forth, and even
forevermore."*
–Psalm 121:8 (NIV)

We have great memories of our time in Turkey as we
were able to visit some amazing places while we were young.
Our travels would never have been possible if Gary hadn't
been sent to Ankara. We visited the different Mosques and
sights in Istanbul. We shopped in the Grand Bazaar, which
is unbelievable, as it is one of the oldest and largest covered
markets in the world. There are sixty-one different streets in
it and over 4,000 shops. It's easy to get lost when trying to
see everything. This was a great experience because we were
treated well by the shop keepers where we purchased special
items.

Another place we traveled to was Princes' Islands of
Buyukada, across the waters on the Bosphorus. We took a fer-
ry from Istanbul that crosses the Sea of Marmara. Buyukada is one of the nine small islands, which make up the Princes' Islands. This beautiful island is car-free, so horse-drawn
carriages (phaetons) are prevalent as they pass the homes
along the tree-lined streets. The air is intoxicating with sweet
smelling magnolias, mimosas, tangerines, and lemons. To us,

it seemed like a fairy tale.

We went to Izmir and saw the Whirling Dervishes Ceremony, which began in the 12th Century. The dance is a religious ritual and meditation, focusing on an inward search for God. The dancers are dressed in white, long flowing skirts and wear a tall camel hair hat. The dancers spin around in a large circle to music that leads them into hypnotic states and trances, which can last for hours. There are different parts of the dance to illustrate a story, symbolizing the blessings of God. To be in the presence of it is a fascinating sight. To learn more, you can watch it on the Internet.

We also were able to go to Athens, Greece, and climb the Acropolis up to the Parthenon, as well as to see other sights around Athens. It was all an unbelievable experience for us, and we did not take any of these traveling blessings for granted. We never have forgotten who our God is and that we need to give Him praise and glory always for how He loves us and all He allows us to experience during our lives.

Having the opportunity to live in another country outside the United States was a real eye-opener and faith-builder for us. It was a life lesson that was and always will be priceless to us. I do believe this unexpected assignment gave us more of an education about life than we ever could have learned by attending college classes. I am forever grateful for God's hand in this journey that began Gary's and my life together. We know it is what helped shape us from the beginning. We grew up and became responsible people. We learned not to take anything for granted but to always appreciate and be thankful for what is happening in each step of our lives. We witnessed the struggles others in different countries have.

In many cases, people possess so little, but they still find ways to be thankful and happy with what they have. The way they live puts into perspective how blessed we are in the United States.

Stories are read about things people have to do to feed their families, but until you observe it with your own eyes, it really doesn't register most of the time. There were men with no legs on the side of the street, struggling to get around and begging for money to buy food because no one would give them a job. Poorer women went down in muddy holes, sometimes so deep only the top of their heads could be seen, as they were digging with picks and their fingers to collect any pieces of coal that they could find to start a fire to keep their family warm. None of this is a joke. It was happening then, and in parts of the world, those same things still happen, as well as many other heartbreaking struggles to survive. These things happen in our own country, and we ignore them way too much. I feel blessed that at eighteen and nineteen years of age, Gary and I were placed in a position where we could learn through real life experiences to always be thankful and strive to help others we see who need our help, no matter how little or how much we can do. We try to never forget that even when we feel we are struggling, there are always others that are struggling more.

I left Turkey right before Gary was scheduled to end his tour there and went to stay with his parents until he returned to the States for a visit before going to his next assignment. Gary would be spending his last two years of service at Wright Patterson Air Force Base, located just east of Dayton, Ohio.

We found an apartment to rent in Fairborn, Ohio, just a mile from the base. We enjoyed our time there; having a base close by made it nice to enjoy all the benefits available for military families.

Gary was offered a promotion and a bonus along with a great tour of duty in Germany if he chose to stay in the Air Force a couple more years. We had become good friends with another couple while at Wright Patterson Air Force Base. They decided to extend their service two more years and were able to travel all over Europe from Germany. I'd gotten a real taste for traveling while overseas and wanted to see more. So, I was all for going to Germany for a couple more years and encouraged him to accept the opportunity.

Once again, as when Gary had experienced the urge years ago to volunteer, which sent him to Turkey instead of Vietnam, he must have experienced the urge to decline and return to our home near Cincinnati and be close to family again. This decision would prove to be what was best for us at that time. If we had gone to Germany, it would have been a decision we would have lived to regret and feel guilty about for many years to come.

"The Lord himself goes before you and will be with you; He will never leave you nor forsake you. Do not be afraid; do not be discouraged."
--Deuteronomy 31:8 (NIV)

Gary is shown here standing at
parade rest and positioned with an
M-16.

Gary and I touring the Island of Aegina
in Greece, 1968.

Gary standing in front of Sultanahmet
(The Blue Mosque) in Istanbul, Turkey,
1969.

CHAPTER 11: Returning Home – Heartbreak and Happiness

"Many are the afflictions of the righteous: but the Lord delivereth him out of them all."
--Psalm 34:19 (KJV)

Upon our return home and getting settled, Gary began working as a Deputy Sheriff with the Hamilton County, Ohio Sheriff's Department. With his experience as an Air Police, it was a good step for him into the law enforcement field. We moved into a home that his father had built years ago, and it was right next door to where his father and mother were living. We had no problems with being next door; we always got along great and appreciated them allowing us to live there while making the adjustment from military life.

Gary's father's health seemed to be changing. More often, he wasn't feeling well, which was unusual for him. He had always been a healthy and hearty man, always keeping busy, working hard, and enjoying being with his family. Gary and his father were so close, and it would have really been hard for Gary if he hadn't been around to do what he could for his father if we had gone to Germany.

We all realized that he didn't seem to be improving and knew it was time to see a doctor. When he was diagnosed with late-stage lung cancer, his health declined very quickly after that. Our living next door was a blessing for us. We'd be right there to help his mother and be able to spend all the time we were able to with his father.

His father was also able to meet our first baby, a little girl, who was born on July 6, 1971. He was a Pawpaw that any grandchild would be thrilled to have. He loved all his grandchildren with a passion, and smiles did not leave his face when any of them were around. And this little girl of ours was the first grandchild that his son and wife had. This made her very special to him.

He was able to hold Lori, his new little granddaughter, and give her as many hugs and kisses as he could. He loved the color red, and when she was wearing a red outfit one day, he was delighted and called her Pawpaw's Little Red Bird. The time he got to spend with Lori was not enough for him, I know, but he delighted in each moment he had with her. On November 14, 1971, just nine days before his sixty-second birthday, he left his earthly body and was at home with the Lord.

Our little girl was just four months-old and would not have the privilege to know the grandfather who would have always made sure she knew how much she was loved by him. Gary and I were twenty-three years old, such a young age for a son to lose his loving father. It was and still is sad that his father could not be around to share more of our life. We were where we were needed to be because Gary followed the path that was laid out before him as revealed by our Lord. We were spared from the guilt we surely would have carried if we had been away and not home during this time. God knew we would be needed, Gary had been able to spend some precious time with his father, and he'd be able to comfort his mother when she was left alone without her husband, whom she had shared every moment since they were married.

Our baby girl who was born that July was perfect in every way. She helped to give us all some joy in our time of sorrow. Her 7lb 7oz weight was just right to make her a dainty baby girl. She had big bright brown eyes and silky blonde hair on her tiny head. We named her Lori Beth (no, not after Lori Beth Cunningham on the popular TV show, *Happy Days,* for those of you who remember watching it) because we liked the name Lori. Her middle name was to honor my mother in a small way. Her name was Betty, and we really didn't want to call her Lori Betty, which wasn't as cute as Lori Beth. Mom was happy with us naming her Beth, grateful we had tried to include her name. We were so happy to have this precious child, God's gift to us, after four years of marriage.

My pregnancy had been a breeze. I only gained around eighteen pounds and felt great all the time. I was full of energy and able to continue doing all the things I had done before becoming pregnant. It did not slow me down at all. Best of all, I never had morning sickness and was happy to finally be having our first child. I was living a life of leisure, not working now. I enjoyed keeping house, cooking, and sewing maternity clothes formyself. I made almost everything I wore during my pregnancy. I loved to sew and make whatever I could.

When the days outside were nice, warm, and sunny, I would pamper myself and take the little blow-up baby's pool I had bought and fill it with water from the hose and just sit in it and relax like a duck in water. I could sit there and read while I relaxed. I had the best tan of my life from sitting out in that little baby pool.

In the '70s, ultra sounds weren't used unless there were issues, so we didn't know if we were having a girl or a boy. I couldn't get all excited about shopping for strictly pink or blue things like most parents-to-be would do, so I just got a few things here and there that could be considered okay for either a boy or a girl, like yellow and green. Disposable diapers were not really used much at first, so we stocked up on cloth diapers, hoping not to have to constantly do laundry. The washer and dryer were located in the basement, which had steep steps down to them. Gary's mother had fallen down the steps once when they lived in the house. I was fearful I might do the same if I were hurrying around. With a new baby on the way soon, I didn't want to be in a position I couldn't get up and get to her if something happened while Gary was at work. I made sure to have a supply of diapers that would last a few days and to have a good diaper pail for soaking the diapers, so they wouldn't stain. As another precaution, I usually did the laundry when Gary was home.

We were really thankful for the four years of our marriage and our time together and our experience overseas – but we were more than ready to begin our family. Fortunately, Gary happened to be home when my water broke, so we grabbed the bag we'd packed, called the parents, and left for the hospital. We'd taken a test run a couple of weeks before to determine how long it would take to arrive at the hospital when the big day arrived. We were impatient to get there and discover if we were parents of a son or daughter. Our trip was safe; all was going well.

After completing the necessary paperwork for admittance, we were led to a labor room. We telephoned family and promised to keep in touch and let them know when the doctors said the baby was definitely making his/her way into the world. I was optimistic all would go like clockwork and be quick and easy. Besides, everything had gone smoothly so far. We would have our little bundle very soon. I was having the normal labor pains, nothing really, really awful, but they were happening. I thought, not long now.

I couldn't have been more wrong. We waited and waited. Each time I was checked I was told I wasn't dilated enough to deliver. We had been instructed to come to the hospital when my water broken because that was the first stage of labor, but I needed to wait. Everything will progress. They will continue to check on me and will have me in the delivery room in time for birth. I'm not too worried. Gary and I continued to wait. While we talked, I used my breathing exercises whenever it was necessary to overcome a contraction. I wish we hadn't come so soon. I'd rather have waited at home. It's boring in this room. There's nothing interesting to keep us entertained, plus I can't even eat anything, and I'm really hungry. I sure didn't expect birth to go like this after feeling so great during the nine months of pregnancy. I expected this to be a piece of cake, too.

I certainly never dreamed of being in labor for twenty-three hours! That was how long we were stuck in that room before they finally announced it was time to go and have a baby. I knew Gary had to be relieved because of my testiness when he was trying to make things better, but his attempts failed to help as the labor became harder. It's interesting how labor pains just seem to turn you into a different person that who you normally are. Mothers reading this book can certainly relate to what I'm saying. I became more vocal than normal and didn't seem to appreciate anything Gary tried to do or say to be nice and assure me all was well.

Finally, I was given an epidural, which I profusely thanked them for. Then they situated me, so I could watch this little baby making an entrance right before my eyes. I was more than ready. I have always been one who likes to know what is going to take place during any kind of surgery and watch, if possible.

Gary is not quite the same. Even though he was a deputy sheriff at that time, he had not helped with the birth of a baby, and he really didn't want to watch his wife in pain any longer, let alone watch our baby being born while looking in a mirror the way I would be watching it all. Or maybe he just needed to be away from me for a while after listening to me for twenty-three hours! I really couldn't blame him. Actually, it wasn't common practice for husbands to be present in the delivery room during those years. It had just started being allowed in the '60s, but a lot of men still were not crazy about watching. Wives just figured they would faint and get in the way, so I was fine with him not being in the delivery room.

I was thrilled to watch it all, especially since I wasn't feeling any pain. It was such an awesome experience to watch my first child being born. I still have the image clearly stored in my mind. I saw that perfect little head making its entrance into the world. I watched with amazement and love as she slowly turned her head from side to side, as if she were checking out this open new space. She had been confined inside a cozy, warm, and familiar place for so long.

Instantly, I was overwhelmed with a new type of love

for this child, this true blessing from God. The immediate connection led straight to my heart. It was a feeling I'll never forget. Those heart strings were strong, and they have remained strong to this day.

The mother-daughter relationship is something I cherish always, maybe more than some other relationships because I never felt my mother and I had that same kind of closeness. It's very special to me to have a loving relationship with my beautiful daughter. Even though she is truly a Daddy's girl, I know we have that special mother-daughter connection, so that is good for me. I was a Daddy's girl too, so I understand.

After several days, it was time to go home, so I was grateful. When Gary arrived to get us, he had a carrying seat (no car seats like now) and the cutest "going home dress," which he'd shopped for. She settled in the carrier and slept. On the way home, we stopped at Mom's house so Grandma could meet her precious great-granddaughter. Lori looked like a living baby doll. Obviously, we knew she was the cutest little girl there ever was. Her daddy had done a great job selecting just the right dress in the whole mall. I pictured him going into every store until he found the perfect dress, so he could show off his daughter. After all, she was Daddy's little girl.

"Just as a father has compassion on his children, so, the Lord has compassion on those who worship Him."
--Psalm 103:13 (AMP)

CHAPTER 12: Joys of Parenthood

"Behold, children are a heritage from the LORD,
the fruit of the womb a reward."
--Psalm 127:3 (ESV)

Lori was a sincere pleasure to watch as she grew from baby to toddler. We had fun as we witnessed her personality beginning to develop more. It seemed our daughter was always happy and smiling; she didn't have temper tantrums like other children I'd see when we were out and about around others. It's sad we didn't have a way to record her actions and her voice when she was growing up, so we could go back and watch it again and again. Hearing her little voice and the cute things she'd say as she played just filled my heart with joy.

My love for sewing was perfect for making little girl clothes. I made most of her toddler-sized clothes, always finding the cutest fabric and making adorable girlie things for her to wear. She would catch people's eyes as she walked around all dainty and cute in her outfits. They'd give her big smiles, which she always returned to them. Lori was our little *Shirley Temple*, only cuter of course. Those years flew by too fast. I would love to re-live her first four years of life over and over, soaking in every second, so I'd never forget anything. But as we age throughout the years, our memories lessen and fade, but I still can feel so much in my heart where I know it will last forever. This little girl, who was given to us as our

This is a picture of our precious
little girl, Lori, age four.

first child by God, and the special help she would be to me in the following years just confirm the words I read, "Children are a Gift from God." The Bible clearly states children are to be looked upon as a blessing, not as an inconvenience.

My heart breaks when I hear parents complain about how their children are cramping their style. They aren't taking seriously the fact they are a blessing from God, a gift He chooses for us to receive. I would gladly unwrap that gift and receive it with joy and love over and over if it were possible. Even if it meant twenty-three hours of hard labor.

Gary and I had planned to try for another child when Lori was about a year old because we wanted our children to be close, playmates, and have fun growing up together. I always observed families with several children, and it seemed they enjoyed each other. Certainly, this isn't always the case, but the ones I knew seemed to love being from a large family. We kept trying even though the doctor had told me it might be hard for me to get pregnant again. I didn't take it seriously because we had no problem getting pregnant the first time when we decided to try after I had stopped taking birth control pills.

But the doctor was right. It took over three years for me to get pregnant. Of course, we were thrilled to learn we were going to have another child. Maybe it would be a boy this time. At least we'd have two children if not the big family I'd dreamed of. At the time, I didn't understand why it was taking so long to get pregnant, but now, I know it was all part of God's plan in our life, and it was all done in His perfect timing.

I was ready for this pregnancy to be just like it had been when I was carrying Lori, feeling good the entire time, and continuing my normal routine with ease and energy. But, was I in for a different experience!

This time I was sick from the beginning, had no energy, and kept gaining weight up to the tune of sixty-five pounds! This baby just had to be a rotten little boy. Gary had been a big baby; he weighed almost twelve pounds when he was born. Lori's perfect birth weight of 7 lbs., 7 oz. had not made me sick one single day, so of course, I was blaming all my discomforts on the male gender. But one thing I did know – I was NOT going to spend twenty-three hours in the hospital waiting for this baby to be born. I'd rather feel miserable at home instead of being in labor at the hospital and stuck in a small room for hours.

I felt like a big barrel. No longer could I get down on the floor to play with Lori. Otherwise, I'd be rolling around on the floor, unable to stand. After Gary returned home from work, he would struggle to lift me if I did get on the floor to do anything. Along with feeling miserable, I was grouchy, which I didn't enjoy. I hated myself this way. I even told Gary in an unkind way, "I will not go to the hospital until the pains are so close that I know the baby is going to be born soon. I have better things to do than sit in a room forever with nothing to do but focus on my pain."

Needless to say, Gary was not crazy about the idea at all. The hard part for him was with being on the sheriff's department, it meant he always worked different hours and covered different territories. He never knew how far from home he might be when I decided I was ready to go. He didn't want to be in a situation where we didn't have time to have someone here for Lori and not arrive at the hospital in time. It was reasonable and practical for him to think this way, but grouchy me wouldn't have it. I was waiting!

On November 23, 1975, Gary was dressed in his uniform and ready to serve a midnight shift. I was experiencing some labor pains, but wasn't ready to go, so I told him to go ahead to work. Keep in mind, we didn't have cell phones in 1975. It wasn't easy to call and ask him to return home. Thankfully, my sanity suddenly returned, and I realized I should go ahead to the hospital before he had to end up delivering the baby along the side of the road somewhere. Just in time reasoning knocked me over the head as he was walking out the door.

"Gary, maybe you should stay home."

Thank the Good Lord my sanity returned when it did. After Lori's care was assured and she was settled and safe, we headed to the hospital. My contractions were really close, but I tried not to demand Gary step on the gas --- speed up the car – put the pedal to the metal – it was I who had caused this trip from being nice and calm. But I didn't try to stifle my screams. I thought I was doing Gary a favor by not making him spend so many hours, hearing me carrying on in the labor room like I'd done years before with Lori. My poor husband!

When we parked at the hospital doors, he ran and got a wheelchair and pushed me in quickly. "This baby is coming soon."

I must have been making some pretty crazy noises. Either that or my face was showing pain and panic when we got to the reception desk. Before what seemed like a second, I was being whisked away before Gary had time to say anything else. He stayed and completed the paperwork before returning outside to park the car. I noticed from the wall clock we passed on our way to the delivery room that it was midnight. I heard my doctor's name being called over the speaker and

STAT!

Gary didn't make it to the delivery room in time. Obviously, we'd barely made it into the delivery room. I'd told everyone I wasn't spending twenty-three hours in a labor room and I didn't. Unfortunately, my stubbornness had resulted in not having time to get an epidural to ease my agony. I was too busy yelling about the pain to watch the little head come into view and greet the world like I'd done when Lori was born. I did hear the baby cry in between my loud screams, so I was thrilled and thankful to know the baby was okay. At ten minutes after midnight, I'd given birth to a baby boy, which I knew he would be. But I could not stop insisting to anyone who would listen that I was still experiencing terrible discomfort.

"I keep my eyes always on the Lord. With Him
at my right hand, will not be shaken.
Therefore my heart is glad, and my tongue
rejoices my body also will rest secure."
--Psalm 16: 8-9 (NIV)

CHAPTER 13: God's Gift of Yet Another Baby

"God blessed them and said to them, 'Be fruitful and increase in number; fill the earth and subdue it. Rule over the fish in the sea and the birds in the sky and over every living creature that moves on the ground.'"
–Genesis 1:28 (NIV)

After the doctor and nurses checked everything regarding the baby, they told me he was okay. "The baby has been born, so you will be fine." Obviously, they thought because I hadn't been given anything for pain, I was just being over-dramatic about the pain and wanting empathy. Well, it was left to me to convince them this pain was not going away. So politely (well, okay), not politely but very loudly I insisted they do something --- NOW! The medical staff must have surmised, she isn't going to calm down. We better take another look so she'll quiet down. But women know our own bodies.

As the doctor was taking a second look, he almost yelled, "Give her an anesthetic quick!" '

I was relieved and thankful when the pain eased, and I began drifting off. In the fog between reality and dreamland, I faintly heard someone say, "It's another boy!"

As I entered blissful sleep, I thought, *Oh, how sweet!*

Another lady must have delivered a little boy like me. Our babies will have the same birthday.

Have you figured it out? I did not have just one rotten little boy; I had two rotten little boys. (They were never rotten, that's just how my stubborn and barrel-feeling self was thinking before they were born.) The big 12-pound boy I imagined having was actually 5-pounds and 5-ounces and a second boy weighing 5-pounds and 11-ounces. I was almost right about the weight. What a big surprise we received that night and one we would never have imagined.

Not only were Gary and I both shocked, but the doctor was, too. He was surprised my yells weren't because I enjoyed drama, but because there was another little guy making his way into the world ten minutes after his brother. And their poor Daddy had missed it all!

I was somewhat unaware of the subsequent events before I was wheeled into the recovery room. I may have been a nuisance in there while I was waking because each time I came to a little, I asked, "Excuse me! Did they say I'd had twins?"

The duty nurse answered sweetly each time, "Yes Honey. You did have twins – little boys."

Then I'd drift away into heavenly slumber. The number of times I awoke and asked the same question before dozing off is unknown, but it must have become annoying for the kind nurse. When I awoke again, I didn't finish, "Excuse me," before the nurse replied not so sweetly but loudly, "YES! YOU HAD TWINS!" That shut me up.

In a gentler voice, she assured me the babies were being given good care, and I'd see them soon. After thanking God for the blessings of two baby boys, I decided to enjoy the rest and sleep while I could.

When I awoke and saw Gary, I was impatient to hear his rendition of the exciting events that evening. Of course, he was shocked, too. The doctor had said, "Congratulations! You have a baby boy. He's a little small, but there is a reason for that."

Gary's excitement for having a son turned to worry, but the doctor quickly added, "That's because there are two little boys. You have twins!"

When the doctor held up two blue cards with Baby "A" Kilgore and Baby "B" Kilgore, Gary laughed from relief. Maybe the doctor was trying to convince Gary and maybe himself by holding up those little blue cards. He told Gary he was as shocked as us about there being two babies.

What a night for us when those two little boys made their entrance into this world. Forever, I'll call it the night of our miracle from God. In His omnipotence, He knew because of tonight, a life would be saved years later.

We didn't have an inexperienced doctor, just limited equipment in the '70s. Wonderful pictures of the babies in the womb were not available like today. We couldn't see how the baby was developing, if the baby was in distress, or if we were having a boy or girl or more than one baby. One thing is for sure: I would have been at the hospital long before birth if I'd known I was having twins. I'd ensure there was time for an epidural or spinal block and the magic of no pain before Baby "A" was even thinking about entering the world. My lesson learned was no more waiting to get to the hospital if I were ever to give birth again.

The doctor's theory is the boys probably surrounded

each other when he listened for the heartbeat. He'd never heard two different heartbeats – only one at each examination. To illustrate so I could understand, he made a fist and wrapped his other hand tightly around his fist to make a ball. He was an excellent doctor, one of the top obstetricians / gynecologists in Cincinnati. Women were hopeful of getting appointments with him. I'd been fortunate twice as he was the same doctor to deliver Lori. We'd later learn the unusual situation of this birth was a rare occurrence.

At an acceptable hour, Gary telephoned the family to announce our news. We'd been in such a rush to leave we hadn't called them before. After all, there was no reason to wake everyone, knowing it might be hours again before the baby was born. And our suspicions were correct. No one believed Gary when he said "twin boys." Always the jokester who enjoyed making family members laugh, they assumed he was telling another story. It took a while to convince them. Then Gary couldn't resist announcing our difficult time naming the boys.

"What do you think? Frick and Frack? Tom and Jerry? Burger Chef and Jeff? Or maybe Mutt and Jeff sound better. They were relieved to hear Baby A was Jacob Steven Kilgore, and Baby B was Jason Stuart Kilgore.

Thankfully, the Kilgore name would continue into the next generation and more to come in the future. Gary and I were happy to do our part. It's such a great Scots-Irish name. (I'm happy to tell you now that two of our four grandsons have the surname Kilgore.) We'll pray for one of the grandsons to be blessed with boys, so the name will continue.

"I will give you hidden treasures, riches stored in secret places, so that you may know that I am the Lord the God of Israel, who summons you by name."
--Isaiah 45:3 (NIV)

Gary with our newborns, Jason and Jacob (Jake) when both of them were finally home in time for Christmas 1975.

CHAPTER 14: Going Home

"Now may the God of hope fill you with all joy
and peace in believing that you may abound in
hope by the power of the Holy Spirit."
--Romans 15:13 (NKJV)

It was time for me to be discharged to go home, usually a happy day for new parents, but it wasn't joyful for us. Both babies had to remain in the hospital in incubators a while longer because they were small and born a little early. Before ever holding them in our arms, we'd be leaving them behind. Jason had respiratory problems and was jaundiced and bruised all over his tiny body. Both babies were being fed by tubes and continually being monitored to check their vitals. Along with needing to grow stronger and gain weight before they could come home, they needed to develop their sucking reflex to ensure they were getting enough to eat.

It was difficult leaving them there with all the tubes and machinery surrounding them. Somehow, they looked even tinier and more vulnerable that they actually were. We both experienced such an empty feeling as we left without them, but knew it was necessary for them to receive the special care that they would need. But it was still heartbreaking to walk to the car without them. We'd been blessed by God and trusted that He'd given us two babies for a reason. We had faith that soon they would be healthy and able to come home to meet their sister who was anxiously waiting to welcome her baby brothers.

Gary and I visited the hospital as often as they allowed to check on our babies and just to be able to see them. After a week Jacob, Baby "A", was stronger and moved to the regular nursery. That was a great day! We scrubbed, got into gowns, and were led to the nursery. Finally, we were holding one of our tiny boys. Jacob's little head fit in the palms of our hands. He was so fragile, we feared we might break him like you might break a thin sheet of glass if not extra careful. We spent time holding him and rocking him. I thought of Lori, who had not been a big baby – just a little over seven pounds – and the difference of just a couple pounds between her weight and the boys was so dramatic to feel.

It was probable Jacob would come home before Jason. Jason needed the incubator a little longer. Then he'd be moved to the regular nursery for further monitoring before he was strong enough to come home. During the times when you feel let down by certain circumstances, if you stop and reflect on them, you will usually find something good that will take place because of it. Maybe it happens soon after the hard time or disappointment. Maybe it happens years later when you can recognize it led to a blessing you could not consider when you were going through it. Looking back, we could recognize the importance of leaving the boys after their birth.

When you do reflect on your difficult times, some may seem silly; some may seem important. But I believe every step of the way is an important lesson that reminds us our path is one our Lord in Heaven has mapped for us and will lead to what is best for us when we allow Him to be in control of our lives. The surprise of having two babies left us unprepared at home, as you can imagine.

So, we definitely needed to go shopping, even if it was a wintry December day with the cold wind cutting through you. Every intake of cold air felt as if your lungs would freeze. After bundling Lori, we began our excursion to the mall. Shopping with just Lori was a blessing. Holding her hand was more pleasant while we searched for all we needed. We could imagine what our future would be like with the twins. We'd be carrying everything but the kitchen sink when we went out with them.

We needed bassinets and another crib, but we decided on buying two new cribs. Lori's wouldn't work; it was white and girlie. Besides, didn't we need two alike? "Yes," we agreed. "They had to be matching for sure." A nice saleslady offered to help, so we told her we were looking for boys' baby cribs. She asked, "When is the baby due?" Bless her heart, (as we say in the south) I could've been hurt, but I wasn't. The sixty-five pounds wasn't magically going away as the eighteen pounds had after Lori was born. My belly looked as if another baby could still be in there. "The babies have already been born."

She looked mortified and searched for something to say. I felt bad for her and tried to make light of the situation by explaining my weight hadn't dropped, but she was so embarrassed, she found it difficult looking at me. Gary rescued us by sharing the events of the night they were born. He even began with my stubbornness about not leaving until it was time for the baby to be born. He told about the surprise of having twins and how he missed it all. Then, of course, threw in his suggestions for their names that he'd told the family. That did it! She chuckled and began to enjoy her day once again.

Lori's cloth diapers were not preemie, so they would swallow the boys. We needed preemie diapers and tiny rubber pants. Thankfully, Dad gave us a case of disposable diapers we could use later when they were big enough. That would be great! We couldn't use many baby items we'd kept of Lori's. So, it was fun buying two of each outfit we couldn't resist. Lori thought we were buying clothes for her small baby dolls.

Our shopping trip was a success as we purchased what we needed before bringing both babies home. Our concerns about having a crib and diapers for both boys had evaporated. We even had enough diapers and outfits, so I wouldn't need to do laundry all the time. We were excited to return home to prepare the nursery. Thank goodness things didn't cost as much back then as they do now.

"But my God shall supply all your need
according to His riches in glory by
Christ Jesus."
--Philippians 4:19 (KJV)

CHAPTER 15: Superfetation

"Now all glory to God, who is able, through His mighty power at work in us, to accomplish infinitely more than we might ask or think."
--Ephesians 3:20 (ESV)

We all get caught up in busyness, trying to accomplish many things. Our minds become filled with planning, causing us to forget things we really wanted to do. This was the case with Gary and me during this time. While planning for the boys' homecoming and traveling back and forth to the hospital, we kept forgetting to set up a time to speak with the doctor. We had questions about their development. We'd noticed Jacob and Jason seemed very different, not just their size, but their stages of development and how different it seemed for babies born on the same day.

Finally, we arranged to have a special chat with the doctor about our concerns. His explanation was a bit unbelievable. What he told us was foreign; we'd never heard of anything like this. We found it amazing and educational.

"What occurred is called *Superfetation*," he explained. "It is an extremely rare situation in which a pregnant woman becomes pregnant a second time with another (younger) fetus. *Superfetation* is characterized by the fertilization and the implantation of a second oocyte in a uterus already containing the product of a previous conception.

"Superfetation is different from the process of twinning or multiple gestation and involves the conception of an additional fetus during an established pregnancy. With Superfetation, the two fetuses have different gestational ages and due dates. It can occur in some animals, but is extremely rare in humans. Fewer than ten cases have been reported in the medical literature" (*medicinenet.com*).

Our case was not reported, so I know of eleven cases and would guess there are others that haven't been reported. But it's still a rare condition. I'm so thankful I was able to have both babies the same day. Thankfully it was a surprise for the doctor, he may have wanted me to carry Baby "B" longer until he was more developed before being born had he known.

The doctor said, "By observing the twin's different stages of development, it appears Jason (Baby "B") is about three weeks younger than Jacob." This was the answer to our questions and concerns regarding Jason's slower development and the reason for his respiratory problems.

He explained, "Besides the normal complications possible for a preemie being born, there is also the risk of further complications because of Superfetation that include low birth weight, movement and coordination problems, difficulty with feeding, neonatal respiratory distress syndrome (caused by underdeveloped lungs), brain hemorrhage or bleeding in the brain."

Truly, I knew God had bestowed a miracle upon our family in 1975 with the birth of two baby boys. We, along with the medical professionals, were not prepared for two babies, but both were going to be okay. There was no brain hemorrhage or bleeding in the brain. Many years later, this beautiful, life-saving miracle was confirmed. God had chosen the time and place when the miracle would be needed. I will tell you more about it in a later chapter.

When computers became a source of information, my curiosity led me to research more about superfetation to learn all I could about it. According to an article in the *American Journal of Obstetrics and Gynecology,* "While proposed cases of superfetation have been reported in humans, the existence of this phenomenon in humans has been deemed unlikely" (McNamara, et al.). But as I read further the article stated that a "2008 French study found evidence to suggest that superfetation is a reality for humans, but it was so rare that there were only about 10 recorded cases in the world" (Pape).

On the Website, healthline.com, there is an article on superfetation. I learned three things need to happen for this rarity to occur in humans.

1) Ovulation must occur while a woman is already pregnant.
2) Sperm must somehow make it past the mucus plug.
3) Implantation must occur in a uterus that is no longer prepared for it.

I guess that explains why they thought it was unlikely to happen in humans. The truth is those of us who believe in the Almighty God know when something is God's will for us, it can most certainly happen. He never fails us. He knows exactly what we will need and exactly when we will need it. His timing is perfection! He has our whole life planned, and if we don't mess it up, all things will go according to His divine plan.

Gary and I did try to have more children after this miracle birth for us, but God knew I would not get pregnant again, so He provided two sons in the way He knew would be possible. Our God is an Awesome God!

This is a verse in the Bible that I cherish. Only God can do what this verse says and only God knows what He can accomplish through it. Doctors and scientists can study, speculate, write articles, and think they have all the answers, but it is only by God's hand that the real truth is known.

> *"You made all the delicate, inner parts of my body and knit me together in my mother's womb. Thank you for making me so wonderfully complex! Your workmanship is marvelous – how well I know it."*
> *--Psalms 139:13-14 (NIV)*

CHAPTER 16: Now There Were Three – Help!

"Do not be anxious about anything, but in every situation, by prayer and petition, with Thanksgiving, present your requests to God."
--Philippians 4:6 (NIV)

It was important to me that we arrange the nursery furniture so I could touch both babies at the same time to pat them or comfort them when they were falling to sleep, and when I changed one, I could easily lay him down and lift the other baby without taking a step. We figured the placement of furniture like pros and were amazed how our plans had come together. This was going to be a breeze.

Having time before the boys came home was another blessing, which allowed us to spend special one-on-one time with Lori. I was concerned that with her being the only child for four years that this big change might make her feel left out or neglected. I didn't want anything to change her from the sweet, loving little person that she was. We knew the babies would require much of our time, so she needed extra cuddles and explanations about how life would change with two new babies in the family rather than just one. We showered her with assurance she was and would always be the one special little girl in our lives. Nothing would ever change that; we'd always be here for her, loving her forever and that she held a special place in our hearts.

My worries were needless. Lori would prove to become even more sweet and loving. When her brothers came home, she was the helping hand and support I needed more than I had realized. Her disposition was a great reminder not to dwell on the negative side of things. What is going on will pass; what is ahead will become something you'll realize has a wonderful positive side to it. That is, unless you miss it feeling sorry for yourself or complaining incessantly.

When things seem confusing or you're feeling uncertain, a positive outlook will make things easier and more constant. Trust and have faith in Jesus. Let him be in control.

Believe me, I've had to learn some hard lessons about letting go many times. Still on some occasions, I pause and take a deep breath, reminding myself all will be well.

> *"Your Father knows what you need*
> *before you ask Him."*
> *---Matthew 6:8B (NIV)*

Having Lori as our first child was no doubt part of God's wonderful plan in our lives. She was the perfect child for which everyone hopes. She made my first experience as a Mommy just like the pregnancy had been: a breeze, a piece of cake. She was a joy to us in every way. Through the baby and even the toddler stages, she was so pleasant and happy all the time. Because she wasn't a fussy baby, I was well-rested. Lori was a good eater, loved bath time, and enjoyed being dressed. When she started walking, I didn't have to put everything out of reach; she listened well and was just the cutest little thing you ever laid your eyes on.

Lori was a living doll baby, wearing the girly clothes I enjoyed sewing from the precious fabrics I found. Passersby always reacted to her with a smile, which she easily returned. By being our first child, I took tons of pictures and filled multiple albums with them.

When the babies finally came home, I discovered what a huge blessing our sweet daughter was. It was easy to comprehend why she was our firstborn and why the boys came along when she was four years-old and not younger as I had wanted to have more children right away. But God knew three children would be the right size family for us.

When we grew from a family of three to a family of five it made me somewhat apprehensive about my motherly abilities. Gary still worked at the sheriff department, but he wore plain clothes now – not a uniform. There were worries and lots of time when he was away for long periods. His scheduled days off usually were interrupted by court duty, special detail work, completing extra reports, and, of course, any unexpected crisis.

After both boys were home, I would have welcomed an extra pair of hands. Unfortunately, Mom was sick with the flu, and Gary's mother was recovering from a mastectomy she had just undergone. So, it was left for me to care for three children day and night when Gary was working or called in. You might say I just put on my big girl panties and told myself, *I can do this. After all, look how well I've done on my own with Lori.* But I quickly learned I wasn't *super mom* and would need assistance once in a while, especially at first. That's when four-year-old Lori stepped in to help.

From day one, Lori had been an intent observer of everything that involved the care of her brothers. Side by side, she was attentive to her baby doll while I was attentive to my living baby dolls. Intrigued, I watched how carefully she handled the doll, changed its clothes, fed it, and changed its diapers. Amazingly, Lori was becoming a gentle *pro* at caring for her doll's every need.

One day, Lori and I were sitting on the sofa with the boys lying on either side of me. We together had just finished filling their little bellies when the oven alarm sounded: dinner was done.

They were still tiny and not trying to roll over, so I felt safe asking Lori to sit between them while I took the ten to twelve steps from the sofa to the kitchen to turn off the oven and prepare our meal. Without hesitation, she gladly situated herself between them, patting each one gently with her little hands to comfort them. Intuitively, she had realized they needed to know she was there with them.

As I was finishing meal preparations, I heard the babies beginning to fuss a little, and I heard Lori saying, "It's okay. Mommy will be right back. I am here."

As I turned and stepped into the living room, she was holding Jacob against her and supporting his little head as she patted his back tenderly. I refrained from the normal motherly reflex of rushing in and grabbing him from her. Instead, I slowly walked toward her, all the while watching in amazement as my precious four-year-old girl handled the situation. We shared in the excitement of hearing him *burp*.

I thought to myself, *Why would I expect anything less*

from Lori. She was born with an instinct to anticipate what needs to be done in the moment. Then, she just does it naturally. She's done it all her life. Whenever there's a need, she's there to help, especially when someone seems to be in distress. I think about all of the times when I haven't known someone needed help, but she jumped up and out of her seat to be by their side before I could even turn around. Lori's a caregiver, a caregiver for those in need, whether it's a person or an animal. She never hesitates a second to help in those circumstances. Truly, it has to be her gift from God. That fills my heart and eyes with wonder and pride.

From that day on, Lori became the extra hands and feet I needed during those early years with our two baby boys. She was an extra comfort to her brothers when I didn't have a free hand available. She was the present help in my times of need as God knew she would be. She helped me feed and change them – taking care of the living dolls and loving the opportunity to help me and care for the two little brothers she so dearly loved and not just during the day but during the times when Gary was working the night shift and the boys woke early, ready to eat. This requirement was accompanied by loud cries for their bottles. Lori would climb out of bed to come and help me.

During those nights, we'd climb into Gary's and my bed, prop ourselves up against pillows leaning on the headboard with a baby on each of our laps. We held their bottles in their mouths and fed them -- a mother and her four-year-old daughter sitting side by side. One night, Gary returned home shortly after we'd begun to feed them. He saw us both half asleep but doing our best to fill the boys' bellies. He got the camera and snapped a picture of the four of us. It was good he'd arrived when he did because we may have fallen back to sleep before the boys were finished drinking. We'd had a particularly busy day and were both worn out. I love that Gary captured that moment. It was such a sweet moment to look back on with Lori helping that way. It was priceless.

> *"Every good and perfect gift is from above,*
> *coming down from the*
> *Father of the heavenly lights,*
> *who does not change like shifting shadows."*
> *--James 1:17 (NIV)*

The pictures on the following page show the children as they are growing.

Top: Lori and her newborn brothers.
Left to right, Jacob, Lori, and Jason.

Bottom: Lori (6 years-old) and the boys (2 years-old) growing up together.

Left to right, Jason, Lori, and Jacob.

CHAPTER 17: Children's Antics

*"We urge you, brothers and sisters, admonish
the unruly, encourage the fainthearted,
help the weak, be patient with everyone."*
--1 Thessalonians 5:14 (NASB)

As the boys grew, Lori became a little mother hen. She always kept an eye on them, and if they were heading toward danger, she rounded them up. Once they began getting around more and more, they kept Lori and me on our toes. What one didn't think of getting into the other one did. They were developing their own special communication. We'd often hear them laughing like they'd just thought of another hilarious scheme they could pull off. It was funny and cute to hear them.

One memory is permanently planted in my mind. They had been taking a longer than normal afternoon nap and I decided I had better check on them. Too bad they hadn't been loud while they were busy in there instead of sleeping like I thought they were doing. It would have saved me from cleaning up a big mess. If I'd been asked what I thought I might see when I opened the door to their room, there isn't any way I could have predicted the scene in front of me. Undoubtedly, it was the messiest of their antics thus far in their short little lives. They had been so very quiet while being so very mischievous.

There they were: both babies wide awake and standing in their beds. From head to toe, they were greasy and shiny-looking with their hair slicked back and their sleepers covered with goo. The sheets had a good rub down, and the cute animal wallpaper I'd hung on the walls beside their beds was smeared with shiny goo. They were smiling and as happy as could be. They were too cute.

One of them had managed to reach over to get an extra-large size jar of *Vaseline* from the changing table (the one we had wisely angled close between their beds to save me some steps) then somehow, they'd removed the lid and were enjoying the task of covering themselves, their beds, sheets, walls, and anything else they could reach – all while not making a sound. Admittedly, they had been very thorough. Obviously, I'd left the lid ajar, or they were just clever enough to remove it. No matter which scenario happened, those two little guys had accomplished their goal.

I had to laugh at their expressions. Both were grinning, as they seemed certain this was the cutest thing ever, and it would be funny for Mommy to see what they'd done. But it was a time-consuming mess to clean up. I didn't count the many times I had to wash their hair before it felt normal again. The sheets, blankets and sleepers were never quite the same, and the wallpaper remained spotted, but it did stay on the wall, so that was good. It's a memory I always smile about when I think of it.

From that experience, I was careful to ensure the *Vaseline* and other lotions were not within reach of tiny fingers again. Needless to say, the nursery furniture was rearranged so the changing table wasn't close to their beds anymore. It was worth the extra steps necessary to get the things I needed.

Dad loved to hear anecdotes of the boys' daily adventures and would laugh at their shenanigans. He always said, "Gabby, you need to write down all this stuff, so you won't forget it. One day, it could be a great book to make people laugh." He got tickled especially about the silly things these inquisitive little imps pulled off. Comparatively, he'd just known my sister and me as babies and toddlers and then Lori, so he got a real kick out of these two boys. It's too bad I didn't write it down; maybe I was too busy cleaning up their *art* work to take the time to jot things down. It would have been fun to read about the things they did that I no longer remember. I'm certain I'd could get some good chuckles now, not having to clean and just being able to enjoy their antics and reminisces. Those precious times seem like a blink of an eye when I look back.

Lori always considered them as the funniest little boys too. When she laughed, she'd get them laughing. That was one collective sound that was wonderful to hear. To this day, they are and always will be her baby brothers. Sometimes, I get to hear that wonderful sound when they are together, making each other laugh about something silly they've concocted to do or say.

Nothing fills your heart more than hearing your grown children making each other laugh and enjoying being around each other. Our children share great relationships and always look out for each other. As time goes by, my heart is filled more and more when I see the love the three of them have for each other. Needless to say, Gary and I are very proud parents that they have that closeness.

Please cherish the time when your children are growing up instead of wishing they would hurry up and get older. Hold on to each and every moment of the years you are given to share in their lives. They fly by way too fast; it is just a very short time you have together when they are little and look up to you with those eyes of love.

Don't be selfish with the time they need by thinking you deserve more time for yourself. You will have more than enough time for yourself sooner than you think, and then you will be yearning for some time back when they were little again. Believe me, you will miss even the messes at times.

> *"But if anyone does not provide for his own*
> *and especially for those of his household,*
> *he has denied the Faith and is worse*
> *than an unbeliever."*
> *--1 Timothy 5:8 (NKJV)*

Uh oh, caught in the act.
"Oh hi! We thought we'd just stand here and sit
here for a little while."

Jacob and Jason learning to climb.

CHAPTER 18: California, the Good and the Bad

"Trust in the Lord with all your heart,
and do not lean on your own understanding.
In all your ways acknowledge Him, and He
will make straight your paths."
--Proverbs3:5-6 (KJV)

Life isn't going to be exactly how you dream it will be. It's not a fairytale like some seem to think it should be or like TV and movies portray. Thank God for that! Life here is just temporary, so don't waste so much of it worrying and wishing it could be something it's not. Make the best of what it is instead of always asking why it can't be different or like someone else's life.

I can promise there will be good times and bad times, which is also true in the people's lives you look at and envy. Everyone will have ups and downs and hills and valleys -- that's how life is. There is no avoiding the difficulties, but there is a way to handle them, so you can make it to the other side of whatever is going on and learn to be stronger when facing another struggle.

When we choose to allow God to be in control of our lives instead of always fighting what is happening, we will find ourselves looking at things differently. Pray for His will and not ours to be done.

The years passed by until Gary made the decision he didn't want to continue working as a deputy sheriff. Admittedly, I was happy about his decision. Danger wasn't as serious as today for our hard-working, under-appreciated, and under-paid law enforcement officers, but Gary had faced many serious situations that only by God's grace and mercy was he able to safely come home to us after each of his shifts.

But he was affected and experienced difficult times because of things that happened and things he saw. Gary didn't share all of them with me; he spared me, knowing I'd be petrified for him when he was working. When he did share about situations he had to investigate, I could easily see his pain and grief for those involved.

His deciding point occurred when he faced a life-or-death situation. He knows without a shadow of a doubt God was in control that night, and he gives God all the glory for his decision to turn in his badge, not wear a gun on his hip, and leave law enforcement. When facing his own death, he listened to God and didn't pull the trigger. No life was lost that night, but his eyes were opened. He could clearly see he might not have been going home to his family.

"The steps of a good man are ordered
by the Lord...."
--Psalm 37:23 (ESV)

We were thankful to leave law enforcement behind. With three young children, I was relieved not to have guns in the house. Each night I had feared for Gary and the dangerous and disturbing situations he would face. He had joined the sheriff's department because he wanted to help people. He never boasted about being in law enforcement; he was fair and truly cared for those in trouble. I was proud of the honest and caring job he had fulfilled.

Gary worked wherever he could get a decent job to support us, but he continued to apply at different places. Soon, he accepted a position with a well-known air compressor company conveniently located near our home in Ohio. After working a short time, he was excited to be offered a promotion, but his acceptance would mean a life-changing move from Ohio and all of our extended family. With seven-year-old Lori and the boys turning three, we had to decide if we'd move across country to California.

Our family wouldn't be able to watch our kids grow or be an integral part of their lives as they'd been since their births. It would be hard not celebrating birthday parties and holidays together. No more day-long visits or spur of the moment dinners with family or friends. Our children enjoyed spending time with their playmates. We'd miss our church and the different activities for which we were involved with our church family and friends. We'd be leaving life-long friends we'd grown-up with. Lori would start a new school year without her familiar classmates. We knew nothing about California; we'd have to begin a new life on the other side of the country, seemingly so far away from our familiar way of life.

This decision would take much thought and prayer. We asked for guidance and prayer from family, friends, and church family. This was a tough time to leave without the support of family and friends. We'd traveled a few valleys and were uncertain about many things when trying to make this big decision. But after many prayers and discussions, we put our trust in God to lead us in making the right decision for this season of life. Thus, we'd be moving west.

"If any of you lacks wisdom, let him ask
God, who gives generously to all without
reproach, and it will be given him. But let him
ask in faith, with no doubting."
--James 1:5-6A (ESV)

CHAPTER 19: House Hunting -- What a Shock!

"Have I not commanded you?
Be strong and courageous.
Do not be afraid; do not be discouraged,
for the Lord your God will be with you
wherever you go."
--Joshua 1:9 (NIV)

We sold our house quickly, packed our bags and the kids' favorite toys, and said our tearful good-byes. The company would take care of everything involved in making the move. We were like pioneers (Gary, me, and our three children), heading into unknown territory to begin a new chapter in our family's life. At least we were flying from Cincinnati to Los Angeles and not riding in a Conestoga wagon. Talk about a long trip. A long flight wasn't so bad when you thought of the pioneers' way of travel.

While getting ready to board the plane, the scanners detected the boys' plastic squirt guns in their backpacks. The TSA agent opened the boys' backpacks and removed the toy guns. "I'm sorry, but they will not be allowed to take the plastic guns with them onto the airplane."

Of course, Gary and I understood it was for safety reasons, but the twins didn't understand why their toys were taken, so we were left with the difficult task of explaining the rules. When we promised to get new and better ones in California, all was well.

This experience in traveling across the country was the beginning of an education for them. They were able to see the world below and then fly above the clouds.

We were looking forward to not having any cold winter weather like we experienced in Ohio, so this would be one good thing about the move. We told the kids about being able to play outside almost every day and that we would take them to Disneyland, Knots Berry Farm, and Universal Studios and to see the ocean as soon as we could. Of course, all of this made them very happy, especially to know they would see Mickey Mouse and Pluto! For sure, it was going to be quite a different life from where we had lived, but the family had promised they would try to come for a visit. We had that to look forward to, along with the warmer weather. In was all going to be a real change for us in every way.

"For we live by faith, not by sight"
--2 Corinthians 5:7 (ESV)

It was 1978 when we moved to southern California and into a rental house Gary had found in Mission Viejo, California, located close to where his office would be located. The area where Mission Viejo had been developed was a hilly region; the land primarily had been used for cattle and sheep grazing before an urban planner drafted a master plan for part of the area to make it one of the most desired areas to live in Orange County. By 1980 most of the city was completed. It was a great location where you could get to the beach and ocean towns easily. If we didn't want to go to the ocean, the developers had made an artificial lake, Lake Mission Viejo, where we could lay on a sandy beach and swim close to home. It was mostly sunny with only about fourteen inches of rainfall a year. So, the weather was great compared to Ohio weather. It was nice living there before the big boom came to the area. It was like a secret place we had found that not everyone knew about yet.

One problem we did have was the interest rate was almost 19% for a mortgage loan, and the cost of housing compared to Ohio was a shock to us. We only had made $10,000 from the sale of our house when we left Ohio. Trying to find a house to buy was impossible in California with our little down payment. A monthly mortgage payment would be way above our means to be able to afford. The rental house was very nice, but we did eventually want to own our own home again. Gary was told when he accepted the job that we would probably be in California for at least ten years, so we didn't plan to rent the entire time we'd be living there. The cost of living in California was so much higher than living in Ohio.

Just out of curiosity, I recently checked the Internet to learn what the cost of living was currently. Living in the Cincinnati, Ohio, area is 50.5% less than living in Mission Viejo overall, and the median cost of a home is 80% less than Mission Viejo. The Los Angeles / Long Beach areas are 196% higher now than Cincinnati. It was such a difference then and now when comparing home prices.

We had only been in our new home that we sold to move to California a couple of years. It was a great home. We'd built it on a nice big fenced-in lot and had an apartment in the lower level that Gary's Mother lived in. It was a very well-built custom home, but we weren't finding anything similar that we could afford. It did seem renting was in our future for quite a while, which wasn't horrible, of course. We were enjoying the nice house that we could not afford to purchase. It was in a great location to get around to visit different coastal towns nearby. We were on top of a hill and could look down and see the lake in the distance on one side, and we could see snow-capped mountains on the other side; so, we felt blessed in that way. The views were beautiful to be able to look at and enjoy.

It was like a whole new world to us. We were in awe, and we sort of felt out of place at first. Finding a church to attend and being made to feel very welcome there helped us feel better; like we were accepted in the community, and all would be well. The minister at the church was a great man. He and his wife also had two boys that were older now, but he remembered how young boys were, so when our boys acted up, he always got a big laugh watching them. One day when our boys climbed under the pews, he got down on the floor and began playing with them. This made us feel more at ease and less embarrassed. Thank goodness this didn't happen during a Sunday service but when we'd gone to register for preschool. The boys thought it was so much fun.

The Minister and his wife were always happy and smiling, always there for whomever might need help. We loved being part of that caring church family. We made many wonderful friends there and began to get involved in different activities available for the whole family, allowing the kids to make some great friends, too.

The school where Lori would be attending also was close, so I would be able to take her to school every morning before taking the boys to the pre-school they attended a few days each week. They were enjoying making new friends in their schools.

Gary found a 1974 Opal Kadett for the kids and me to get around. It wasn't something I would have chosen, but the price was right, and it became fun for the kids to imagine we were in a cartoon car! It was the most awful color -- a bright chartreuse with a black stripe running along the door from the front to the back. Believe me when I tell you, there was not another one like it in that area. It stood out; there was no way I could have hidden from anyone who tried to find me. But I drove that car everywhere for years and years. The kids and I had lots of fun getting around in it. It was our old, faithful, mean green machine.

We were doing pretty well as time went along. I picked up some handiwork I could do at home, making little dolls and dressing them like different characters for a company, which sold them in gift shops in different cities throughout the country. The little bit helped us make ends meet. Working from home allowed me the ability to pick up Lori from school and the boys from preschool on the days they went. All was good with our family of five; we were a real happy team together.

After a couple of years, we had saved money and the interest rates had dropped some, so we began shopping for an affordable house, knowing it wouldn't be in the same neighborhood where we were renting. The good news was now there were other developments in Mission Viejo with less expensive homes for sale. We met a wonderful lady in the church who was a real estate agent, so we discussed our desire to purchase a house.

After two weeks, she'd found a little house at the northern end of Mission Viejo near the Saddleback Mountain that was available on a lease-to-purchase arrangement. The house the realtor had found for us sat on one of the many hills around the area. We could see homes down the hillside and some mountain ranges to the north. We were excited and noted small changes we could make that wouldn't cost a lot and would personalize it more to our liking. This would be a way we could get into a home without having a large down payment. Mission Viejo ended where this community was built. The main road ran north and south and then turned west at the end; there were no more houses built north of there at that time. Of course, now there are more houses, schools, businesses, and churches, including the Saddleback Christian Church, built going up the mountain side.

Lori would have to change schools, but a new elementary school had been built close by that she could walk to. A few families we knew at church lived in the same neighborhood, so their children could walk to school with Lori. Once the boys began school, they'd be able to walk with them. This was a plus for us.

> *"And my God will meet all your needs*
> *according to the riches of His glory in*
> *Christ Jesus."*
> *--Philippians 4:19 (NIV)*

CHAPTER 20: Losing, but Never Losing God

"Cast your cares on the LORD, and he will sus-
tain you; He will never let the righteous
be shaken."
--Psalm 55:22 (NIV)

In order for the lease purchase arrangement to work for us, we would make a down payment of $10,000 we'd managed to accumulate again. Then we'd begin making monthly lease payments. A portion of the lease payments would be applied toward the purchase price we'd agreed on. These payments would lower the loan amount when we were able to get it transferred to our name. Hopefully, this would only be a few years and interest rates would be even lower. On paper it all looked great – the perfect situation. We were pleased to be investing in what would one day be our own California home. We felt blessed with the opportunity to get into a home we could consider our own. We'd be able to paint, plant shrubs and flowers, and make other enhancements we wanted. We were thankful to our real estate agent for finding a home in this area, as well as the lease purchase agreement that made it all possible.

We enjoyed living in the house even though it was smaller than we were used to, but it worked for us. Gary built a really neat decorative wooden fence dividing the property.

We finally got the cute little Cocker Spaniel puppy I'd planned to get when we were first married. We named her Goldie. The kids had so much fun running around the yard and playing with her. Because we couldn't afford a pool, we had an in-ground jacuzzi installed. It was perfect for the kids to jump in and splash around. Goldie even jumped in with them a couple of times to play in the water. Gary and I relaxed in it too, now that we were all settled in and feeling less stressed about not owning a house as we had for so many years before.

Our plans were to spend our years in California here in a home we were thankful for and would be our own. All the neighbors were great. We made more good friends as time went by. The kids loved being outside in the quiet neighborhood and living in a cul-de-sac with very little traffic. After another couple of years, we were in a position to get a loan on the house and have it transferred to our name. We contacted our realtor and explained our plans. She promised to check different loan companies to find the best rates available. She'd also start the paperwork for the transaction and be back in touch with us. But it was a while before we heard from her. Even so, we trusted she had our best interest at heart. After almost two weeks, she called. Her voice betrayed her; we knew something wasn't right. She began to break the news to us.

Many other buyers like us had used this method to get into their homes. The parties on the other end of the deal had been trusted. All involved had felt safe, and believed everything would proceed as it had been presented, agreed upon, and documented. There were no reasons to doubt. After all, everyone had the signed, sealed, and delivered contracts. But things were not as they seemed.

Our realtor was so upset for us that she actually began crying. She was a good woman who had never imagined anything like this would happen. She even quit working in real estate after all this happened. I was sorry for her and hated that it all happened to her along with us and others like us who had gotten into a house this way.

I chose not to remember the exact terms used to explain the situation to us; probably because by that time, I was a bit in shock. But the bottom line was we were not going to be able to buy this house. The money we had invested up front and all the money for leasing over the past couple of years was long gone with the dishonest people who had taken advantage of us. Yes, we had been scammed!

It was discovered that a group had gotten together and decided to purchase as many lower priced homes as they could in the desirable town of Mission Viejo, knowing there were many people moving there from other states who would not have a lot of money for a down payment. They offered this *lease-to-purchase* program requiring potential buyers to put what money they had down and then make monthly payments to them, stating in the paperwork that they would apply a percentage of the amount paid toward the purchase price of the home.

I believe this could be a good program if working with reliable and honest people on the receiving end of the deal. But this group was not reliable or honest; they were evil, scheming criminals, with no conscious or concern for others. They would make hundreds of thousands of dollars up front and knew most of us would more than likely not be in a position for at least two or three more years until we could get our own mortgages to purchase the houses.

That gave them plenty of time for them to collect a lot of money, probably deposit it into a foreign account where it could not be traced, and then be long gone before any one was the wiser.

Not only did we lose everything we had saved and invested, but we had to move out because lawsuits were being filed; the houses involved had to be vacated. They would be tied up in a legal battle for years to come. We were advised that suing to get back our investment would end up costing us more in legal fees than what we would be trying to recover. With as many clients who would be involved, if there was even a little recovered, by the time the attorneys were paid for all the hours they would be billing, very little would be left to split between everyone, if any. The hard work, cost, and stress of it all would not be worth it in the end. We did know there was no use trying to fight it. At least we could appreciate the attorney was an honest person who was advising us and did not make promises to get money back for us when he knew he couldn't. We had his honesty to be thankful for.

The disappointment wasn't quite over for us. We then found out that the home improvement loan we had taken for the fence, paint, and other items to fix the house, along with the in-ground jacuzzi, would still have to be paid off, even though we had to move out of the house. Having to continue paying for something we'd never enjoy was a hardship. We wouldn't even own it after we did pay off the loan. We were right back at the beginning of it all, only without any savings for the future. We started searching for a home we could afford to pay the first and last months' rent and the current month's before moving in. We were seriously beginning to wonder why we'd been led to California.

CHAPTER 21: God's Plan Revealed

"In their hearts humans plan their course,
but the Lord establishes their steps."
--Proverbs 16:9 (NIV)

This was a real low point in our lives in more ways than one. We definitely felt as if we were in a very deep valley and not seeing a way out any time soon. We felt used, betrayed, lost, angry, hopeless, and we felt we wanted revenge in some way. It wasn't fair? Why did this happen to us? The worse part of it all was we lost our faith that God could get us through this. We made ourselves miserable by allowing the dark force in the world to take over our thoughts and our actions. The devil had taken control, and he thought he had accomplished his goal to turn us away from trusting in Jesus.

I cried and we complained to everyone about how unfair it was and how awful those people were who scammed us and others. Gary and I focused our hatred on those who took advantage of us. We dwelled on thinking there should be some way we could get something back. We bickered with each other, and our attitude reflected on our children. We were failing at being tested to prove how we trusted our loving Father in all circumstances that we might face. We were forgetting about our love for each other and those around us and to love

Jesus as He loved us.

I am ashamed to tell you we hung on to this attitude and continued to fight and make ourselves miserable way too long. We were really making Satan happy by being this way. He was rejoicing that we'd lost our trust in God for a time. God was patiently waiting for us to turn back to Him and get back on the path He planned for us.

We loved the area, it was pretty, and it sounded really good to everyone when you said you lived in Mission Viejo; people were impressed. Why did we feel as if we had to impress others like that? When did it become so important, we were allowing it to make us miserable? Didn't we know we might not be able to afford to stay there?

WOW! Where had our trust, love, and faith gone? We were just going in circles displaying our anger and joining the band wagon, showing, and spreading hate, living on the dark side of life and being miserable about things instead of enjoying the life of love, happiness, and thankfulness we had learned so much about in our younger years.

Why had we forgotten to be joyful even through the hard times. We'd witnessed examples of this when we lived in Turkey. We saw those considered poor and lacked material things did not hesitate to do what was needed to provide for their families. While they did what had to be done, they did it with love and a cheerful heart, knowing they would make it through. They never complained or grumbled about in being unfair.

There is nothing wrong with living in a nice area and having nice things. God really does want that for us if we are deserving of those things in our lives while we are here on earth. But, to deserve more requires putting Him first in our hearts and not being selfish or greedy with our blessings and making *things* our priority or acting miserable when we lack them.

When we finally realized that we were wearing ourselves out with this evil attitude and not making matters any better, while not being a good example for others, we recognized we'd been denying our faith and trust in God. He, through His grace and mercy, opened our eyes and hearts to what we had been doing.

We repented and asked for forgiveness for not keeping Him first in our life and not trusting in him and being patient allowing his will to be done in the situation. He never left us during this time, we were the ones who had turned away from him. All the time we were making ourselves miserable, He waited patiently for us to return to what we knew as the truth. We humbled ourselves and admitted our failures. We realized our transgressions and let go of trying to hold on to what we didn't need or deserve. We were not being true to who we really were. Then, and only then, could God continue leading us on the path of his plan for us. He led us out of the valley we had allowed ourselves to get into by our wrong thoughts and actions. It had been our choice to act this way, and our choice caused us to be miserable.

We made the spirit-led decision we needed to move away from Mission Viejo to another area in California where it would be less expensive for us to live. We had been trying to live beyond our means, and it was not good for us. We immediately started taking drives on Sundays to find an area that would fit our needs. We were led from Orange County to Riverside County. We would not be close to the coast and beaches; we would not be in the center of Orange County where many of the exciting vacation spots were close by; and we would not be in the same church where we felt so comfortable and had many friends. We needed this humbling to find our way again to the life that was meant for us at that particular time of our journey in life as a family.

An area in Riverside County, inland and out toward the dessert areas of California, was advertising some new home developments being built at much cheaper prices than homes in Orange County. The exciting thing that caught our attention was if you had been in the military you qualified for a VA Loan, and that meant you did not need a down payment in order to purchase one of the new homes. They would work to make your payment affordable for you, which was exactly what we needed in order to get one of the construction homes being built that we could afford.

We visited the area over several weekends and found model homes that were being constructed. At the time, the town was called Sunnymead, California. It was in the hills above the town of Moreno in a desert area tucked at the base of the Box Springs Mountain. In years to come, these two towns merged into one town that is now called Moreno Valley, California.

It was totally different from the lush green communities of Mission Viejo. It was not a master planned community with clubs and pools and a beautiful lake with the sandy beach to relax on. There were no modern shopping malls, restaurants, or well-known entertainment venues where you could go spend the day riding rides and having fun or spend the day at the beach. It was pretty much considered as being out in the middle of nowhere, not at all like the desired areas that were closer to the ocean.

There was an Air Force base there that had been built in 1918. Today it is a reserve air base, March Air Force Base. There was a deserted NASCAR racetrack located near the freeway that had opened in 1957. It would later become the site for the first shopping center in the area to be built and would be called the Moreno Valley Mall. (That would be a few years after we moved there.) Shopping of any kind was very limited at the time. We had no cinema to go to the movies or pools to go to swim. This would be a big adjustment for all of us compared to where we had lived the past several years. But, if I'm honest, it was more like we had been used to all our years before when we lived in Ohio. What was there that we needed were affordable homes with no down payment required. We could afford a larger home so each of the kids could have their own bedroom and a bigger yard, too.

Gary would now be able to work from home, so it wouldn't be necessary for him to work at the office as much and drive in the heavy traffic going to Orange County. There also was a smaller airport in Ontario, California, that he could get to without too much driving when he had to travel for business. He wouldn't have to drive farther south to the John Wayne Airport (as it was called then) and all the traffic around Los Angeles. We were beginning to focus on the positive points. More and more, we were getting back to our roots and grateful for what we were able to buy.

The house we decided on was two-story with three bedrooms and two baths, along with a big unfinished bonus room upstairs over the garage. Hopefully, we could eventually finish off the bonus room for the kids to have a nice place to hang out with their friends. There was a nice sized living-dining room area with a pretty open staircase leading up to the top level, and a great kitchenwith a big eat at bar and a den beside it. The fourth bedroom was downstairs with a bathroom that I knew Lori had her eye on, so she would not have to share a bathroom with her brothers any longer. Who could blame her for that? Little boys can be pretty messy!

I loved the lot we were able to select for construction. It was in the curve of the street, which allowed the back yard to fan out with lots of space for the kids to play and enjoy being outside with the dog. What was most exciting for me though was that there was a nice big fenced-in field that backed up to our yard. Horses were there grazing and providing a great window view for me. It was amazing to have horses to enjoy watching and feeding apples and carrots to right in my own back yard. They were not mine, but I was able to pretend like they were!

Each new development had T-shirts, refreshments, and other gadgets to advertise their homes, so the kids had ac-cumulated lots of T-shirts during our weekend hunting trips for a home. That turned out to be a good thing because there were many dirt roads with red dirt around the area, and they managed to get very dirty while playing.

After we vacated the house in Mission Viejo and waited for the new house to be built, we decided to treat ourselves for a couple of months by renting a condo in San Clemente near the ocean. The kids had a wonderful time being on the beach each day; we enjoyed walking around the town. We have wonderful memories of that special Thanksgiving and Christmas we spent there. Before school began back up after the holidays in January, we moved into the Residence Inn at Riverside, so we could drive the kids to school in Sunnymead. We weren't there long before our house was finished, and we could move in.

As one of the first families to move into the neighborhood, we got settled and became familiar with the area. As other families came, it was nice to meet and greet them and their children in the beginning, which proved to be a great experience. We established close friendships as we shared our experiences and what brought each family to the area.

Gary and I had stayed in touch with our former minister at the church in Mission Viejo, and a few of our friends there. We missed them and the fellowship we'd shared in church groups. We remained friends, but the move and the distance caused communication to be less and less over the years; however, the minister stayed in touch.

Soon our eyes were opened to how blessings can come from hard times if we allow God to be in control and keep our faith in Him. Thankfully, he does not give up on us or forget about us like we do to Him at times. He continually sticks by us and leads us to the good He has planned for us even if it sometimes means He needs to knock us down, more, or less, to remind us not to forget that!

*"I know what it is to be in need, and I know
what it is to have plenty. I have learned the
secret of being content in any and every situation, whether well fed or hungry, whether
living in plenty or in want. I can do all this
through Him who gives me strength."*
--Philippians 4:12-13 (NIV)

I recently read the article, "Real Intercession." In addition, my friend, Sandi, commented on the article. I wanted to
share it and her comments with you.

"From Faith to Faith: Daily Devotional: Real Intercession"

*And he saw that there was no man,
and wondered that there was no intercessor
-- Isaiah 59:16a (KJV).*

When someone hurts us, our natural human reaction is to strike
back ... to ask God to clobber them.
But that's not God's way.

I realized that one time when
some relatives of mine got robbed,
I was praying about the situation
and puzzling over it.

"Lord," I began to ask, "why did

You let that happen? Why didn't You just knock that thief over the head when he tried to do that?"

Suddenly, God enabled me to back up from that situation .... When I did that, I knew the answer to my question almost as quickly as I had asked it. It was because of His mercy. God has great, great mercy. Not just for me and my family but for others, too.

Think about that next time someone does you wrong. Instead of asking God to knock that person in the head, like I did, consider the fact that -- as onery as he may be -- he may well have a grandmother somewhere who's praying for him to be saved. Stop and remember that God loved him enough to die for him, that He's longing to pardon -- not punish him. Then you can begin to pray for him instead of against him, uniting yourself with his grandmother (or anyone else who happens to be praying for him). You can go to the Lord for mercy for him and you can go up *against* the devil on his behalf. That's real intercession and it throws the forces of darkness into total confusion. They have absolutely no defense against it. The Lord is looking for people who are bold enough, commited enough to do that. Dare to be one of them. When you're you're to change his life instead. (Copeland 1).

My friend, Sandi, commented on this article. "You know, this is amazing to consider from the other perspective. Because God loves us so much, died for us, and is willing to forgive us countless times, He allows us *choice* to make good actions and even *choice* for us to make bad actions. This is because no matter which we choose, He always has His arms wide open to receive us. Can you imagine being the parent who stands by and allows a child to hit your child and who is able to love and forgive that child? God watches this everyday. This is the amazing agape love God has for all people whom He has created."

CHAPTER 22: The Path of Life Continues

"I said, 'You are my servant I have chosen
you and have not rejected you. So do not fear
for I am with you; do not be dismayed for I
am your God. I will strengthen you and help
you. I will uphold you with my righteous right
hand.'"
--Isaiah 4: 9-10 (NIV)

We received a phone call one day from our previous minister to tell us about how his church and others around the area were working with an organization that had begun planting new churches in areas where there was a need for Christians to have places to meet, hear God's Word, and worship. He had known we were having a hard time finding a new church home in the Sunnymead area. The organization had decided that Sunnymead would be a good area to plant a new church.

We had searched since we'd moved there and visited different churches, all requiring us to drive quite a distance each time, so we were thrilled to hear this area was being considered for a new church plant. When a new church is planted, word of mouth to friends and neighbors is how the growing starts. Christians can meet together and learn from the Bible, share thoughts and concerns, pray together, and worship and praise God. Others will hear about it and spread the word to other friends and neighbors, and the plant will continue to grow. I loved the concept of planting a new church. Gary and I and the kids were all excited to hear this. What a wonderful and exciting development in our area where we could be a part of.

The minister informed us of another couple from the church who had decided to move to Sunnymead. They would be visiting and deciding on a home in the near future. This was a young couple with two small children, and they had been part of the music team at the Mission Viejo church. They both sang, and the husband played the guitar. Their voices blended beautifully; they were so talented. We were excited others we'd known were coming to the area and were wanting to become a part of the new church.

We thanked him for letting us know this great news. We were excited to start meeting other people this way. But he hadn't finished the conversation yet. He explained how churches are planted at the beginning. They didn't locate a vacant store front or start in a school. Instead, people opened their homes and invited friends, family, and / or neighbors to come to share God's Word together, like a home Bible study for all ages.

We liked the idea of it being like a Bible study and that it would probably start in a neighborhood and grow from there, branching out to include others in the community. We asked him where the first meeting was going to be.

He surprised us when he said, "It would be great if you could open your home on Sunday mornings and invite your neighbors to attend."

It was exciting to realize we hadn't been happy about moving to this community, but it would become a place where others could come and learn more about God's Word and His love for us. Being considered for this wonderful opportunity had never occurred to us during the conversation. What an honor to be part of this new church plant! We gladly agreed to open our home to others in this way.

We asked if there'd be visiting ministers from various churches who would come and share a message with us on Sunday mornings. His answer was another surprise.

"Gary, I believe you would be able to do that."

"I don't feel that I'm qualified to do that. I've never studied to be a pastor or teacher."

"Gary, I know you can open your Bible and read the stories written in it for others to hear."

Our former minister showed no concern or doubt. "I know you can lead a prayer of thanks for the fellowship and guide others in learning more about Jesus. When others hear about the meeting, there will be more who are eager to hear about the Bible and what it teaches. They will want to come, too. God guides us through it all when we are seeking to learn and share His Word together."

"As soon as the musical couple moves there," he assured us, "they will come and join you in your home and teach the people new worship songs. You will be able to share the Word of God and sing praises to the Lord. Reading the Word of God and sharing the message in song is a great way for all to learn more about Jesus."

*"For where two or more are
gathered in my name, there I am also."*
--Matthew 18:20 (NIV)

Together, Gary and I could do this. We knew this door
had been opened, and we had been led to move here for this
very reason. Our purpose was to provide a place for this church
plant and be part of getting the Word of God out to others in
this new town that was beginning to grow and grow.

We invited the neighbors we had met, and they all
came that next Sunday morning. The following Sunday they
brought different friends and neighbors along, and each Sunday would find someone else new who had heard about the
house where people were gathering and sharing fellowship
and learning more about Jesus through God's Words written
in the Bible.

Our house had become a church plant, and the plant
was being nurtured and was growing right in our home, the
home we were led to by following God's plan for us. Even
when we tried to ruin His plan with our lack of faith at the
beginning and fought to try to stay where we were, God was
patient until we recognized our sins and turned back to Him,
thus allowing us to be led right where we could be used for His
glory. Now, a very real need in this community was being met
with people coming from all over and starting a new life. And
God had chosen us to be a small part of it, even when we had
stopped trusting Him for a time. This was a blessing we have
always felt so very privileged to be part of and so humbled to
be chosen by Him to do this.

No longer were we living in a way that was making Satan happy and, in turn, making ourselves miserable, but we were living in a way that made God happy. We were very happy and felt much love from those around us and especially felt the love of God for us.

Lori was old enough by then to take the smaller children in a group and read Bible story books to them that told them about Jesus Christ and God and how to love one another.   They spread blankets on the floor in the unfinished bonus room upstairs, had cookies and punch, and listened and learned stories and songs about God. We all looked forward to Sundays. Our kids were always up right away when they heard us moving furniture; they came to help without any hesitation. Our home became more filled each time we gathered to worship.

You have heard it said that God works in mysterious ways. I don't know if it was exactly mysterious that we had lost what we thought we wanted as far as a house in an area we thought we didn't want to leave, but it certainly was an amazing experience for our whole family. We were blessed in a way we could never have imagined as a result of what we had once considered devastating. That was surely the work of our God.

This opportunity would never have become a reality if we had stayed in Mission Viejo. There were many churches already in that community and all-around Orange County. This opportunity was part of God's plan in our life and the path to it was guided by all the circumstances that had happened along the way. So, learn from your hard times. Learn when you feel all is hopeless to keep your faith that God has a plan on the other side of what is going on. Don't get discouraged and allow your joy to be robbed from you. Your story might not be a story like this, but more times than not, when you can look back at something you felt was so unfair or had you asking why it was happening, you will realize the wonderful work that God accomplished through you when you trusted Him and allowed Him to lead you so His will, not yours, can be done.

We continued to be blessed, welcoming more and more people into our home while sharing with them the Word of God. The inside of our house had been filled in every spare inch where we could sit people. Rows of chairs were squeezed in, and people sat on the stairs and even on the floor to gather together on Sunday mornings to hear about Jesus and fellowship together. We grew to having seventy-five plus people each Sunday in our home. Soon we were thinking we'd need to line up chairs in the back yard and figure out some kind of speaker system so everyone could hear and be part of the worship.

We figured it out; we would make it work for all, so they could continue to come on Sunday mornings. Usually, the weather wasn't a problem; it was always pleasant enough to sit outside. There was shade on the patio for those who needed to be out of the sun, and there was always cold water and punch to cool off. We could fill the backyard with more and more people who wanted to come. They were excited about having a place to come and wanted to hear more about our amazing God.

But once again God had the plan already worked out. The next week we received a call telling us that a new pastor had been hired and was willing to come, meet with us, and share a message each Sunday. We learned the organization had already contacted the new elementary school and had an agreement with them to allow our church family to begin using space in the school on Sunday mornings. They would just need a couple of weeks to make all the necessary arrangements. Then we would be welcomed into the building to have our fellowship there.

The new pastor would be arriving in a few days with his family, and they would come and meet with Gary and me before the next Sunday. On Sunday morning, we introduced him and his family to our church family and gave them the good news about having a bigger space to meet in, which would give us even more room and more parking places. This would welcome new people who wanted to attend the service. We would meet at our house a couple more weeks until all the arrangements with the school were completed and approved.

We were so excited about having an ordained minister coming to lead us in worship. Never doubt the timing of God! It was a pleasant surprise when we met the new pastor and his family because they told us they were from Ohio, also. And they knew where Cleves was located! They were from an area not far from Cincinnati and had gone to a high school that was one of our schools' rivals, which our high school football team had played against when we were in high school. Gary had played on the team. The new pastor and Gary hit it off right from the start. They began telling old football stories of back in the day when they both played. They had not played the same years; they were younger than us, but they still had fun talking about the schools and football. What a small world it can be.

While they came to meet with us, they also drove around to search for a home to buy and move into as soon as possible.

Just like us coming from Ohio, it was a bit of sticker shock to see how little money could buy for a home here compared to back home. Even out here away and from the more desired areas of California, the cost of houses had continued to inflate. They were able to find a nice house that met the needs of their family. It was being completed soon and would be available for them to move into pretty quickly. But they would have to make living arrangements for a week or two elsewhere until it was ready to be occupied.

We learned they were going to stay in a hotel for a while. The couple had two small children, a three-year-old daughter and a new son not quite one. Gary and I offered a bedroom in our home, so they wouldn't have to go to a hotel and be stuck in one small room together. But they refused and didn't want to cause any of us to move from our own beds. Unfortunately, the bonus room was not finished, so we apologized. We could have made that a comfortable place if the walls had been finished and it didn't seem so rustic.

I have to brag on those of us who were fortunate to have grown up in the Midwest region of the country, specifically Ohio. I know a lot of people consider Ohio the North, but we know it is actually the Mid-West, like it is identified on maps. I wouldn't want to move back and experience the winters there again, but I am proud to have been brought up there around my elders having good morals, good common sense, and being good examples for us. We learned about giving and receiving, truly caring for others when there were needs, giving without any expectation of receiving something in return, and receiving with true thanks for any help provided when in need. We learned that helping was not a burden but a privilege, never thinking we deserved more than what was being offered. We knew how to respect each other. What a wonderful Christian way to be raised, which, unfortunately, seems not to be the way many are being taught today, along with not having manners and love for all.

> *"Show hospitality to one another without*
> *grumbling. As each has received a gift, use*
> *it to serve one another, as good stewards of*
> *God's varied grace...."*
> *-1 Peter 4:10 –11 (ESV)*

In was easy to tell that the new pastor and his wife had been raised with the same morals, values, and respect for others as we had been. They appreciated all we wanted to do to help, and they felt comfortable with us, knowing they could ask us anything and we'd gladly help in any way we could. They didn't want us to give up our bedroom, but they knew we still wanted to help. So, they asked if it would be acceptable for them to stay in the bonus room even though it wasn't finished.

As they had seen the bonus room, they knew it did have two nice sized sofas, electricity, and air conditioning, just no walls. We kept the floor swept and items dusted because Lori and the younger children used it for the Bible stories and songs each Sunday. There was a small television the kids watched once in a while and lamps. The bathroom in the hall was close and we thought the sofas could be comfortable for sleeping.

They had portable cribs for their children that they had brought from Ohio for them to sleep in at the hotel that they could use, so the sofas could be made up to make in comfortable beds for the adults. The extra space allowed everyone to move around better than just one hotel room, and all of our home was open to them. It became a perfect space for them to spend the next couple of weeks as their home base.

We had a great time with the family while they were in our home: sharing meals, sharing great friendship; having good times; looking forward to the growth of this exciting new church family with the pastor leading us in God's teachings. We became great friends and enjoyed watching each other's children grow. Most importantly, we saw the church family continue to grow through his faith-filled leadership sharing God's love.

Meeting in the elementary school was great and it allowed for more and more attending each Sunday. After just a little over a year, the space at the elementary school was becoming crowded as the area had continued to grow. More and more people were coming to the area. New school, churches, stores, and restaurants were being built. The dusty dirt roads were now turning into four lane streets and by this time Sunnymead and Moreno had merged to make the one city now called Moreno Valley. It was time for a new place to meet for our church and thankfully a new high school was welcoming us in so we could meet in their bigger auditorium to accommodate all who wanted to come for Sunday worship.

Not surprising as the area grew, the congregation grew. Soon, the space in the high school was becoming too small. With the congregations' giving and help from the Christian Foundation, which had been the tool that started this church plant, a loan was obtained to begin building a new church.

It was a glorious day when The Moreno Valley Christian Church opened its doors to welcome more and more people to fellowship together. We had a wonderful celebration, knowing this building was able to meet the needs of all who were hungry to learn more about the God, Who loves them. What a blessing to see and experience.

Although the preacher who came from Ohio has since retired and the church's name has changed to Discovery Christian Church, it has continued to grow both in size and membership with new additions built over the years. This church continues to reach out to all who want to be part of God's family. When I last read about the church on the Internet, it appeared there are between eight hundred and twelve hundred people attending service each week. It is such wonderful news to hear people want to be in fellowship with others who love the Heavenly Father and want to spread the Good News.

Our little family was so blessed to have been a small part of reaching so many people. That privilege was one of the most amazing times in our lives. In our case, it was a true blessing in disguise. We have cherished the lessons we learned. Sometimes you must lose in order to gain and realize what you've lost isn't what was important at all.

*"Commit your way to the Lord; trust in Him
and He will do this; He will make your
righteousness reward shine like the dawn."*
--Psalm 37:506A (NIV)

Picture of the group in our front yard of church plant
– the first group of the beginning of the new church plant
at our home in Sunnymead, California. What a blessing!

CHAPTER 23: You Just Never Know

"We have courage in God's presence, because
we are sure that he hears us if we ask him
for anything that is according to his will."
--1 John 5:14 (GNTD)

We were truly loving life in our new home and with our church family. Venturing out allowed us to enjoy lots of special times in the different areas around us that weren't too far away. One particularly special time I often think about was when our family went to Palm Springs for the weekend. After walking around and seeing the sights, we stopped at an outside café for lunch where a mist of water was spraying lightly, keeping us cool as we ate.

After lunch, we enjoyed swimming in the beautiful clear blue pool at the motel where we were staying. The motel was one of the old-fashioned ones like you might have seen in movies filmed in the '40s or '50s. The cute one-story white motel with bright, colorful trim and well-taken care of landscaping made it fun to pretend you were living back in the days of old. The motel was built in the shape of a big U, with the pool right in the middle. You walked out of your room, and you were at the pool for a nice swim to cool off. It was nice to relax and enjoy the charm of the older days. Making this day even more special was when we drove to the Palm

Springs Aerial Tramway after lunch and rode to an elevation of over 8,000 feet to the top of the mountain covered with snow where it was cold.

We took our parkas, scarves, gloves, and beanies, so we could bundle up before reaching the top. This clothing would keep us warm while we enjoyed building snow men, making snow angels, and having a playful snowball fight.

It was great fun watching the kids being so amazed that they were now bundled up, playing in the beautiful white, cold snow when just a short time before they had been in their bathing suits swimming in the warm pool at the motel where it was actually very hot. This was such a great day for us and one memory we continue to cherish.

On another weekend, we were enjoying a church outing in the town of Yucaipa, California, at a beautiful regional park with a great picnic area and a nice well-kept lake for swimming. Everyone had brought tons of food to share; hot dogs and burgers were grilled. We were stuffing ourselves. The day was beautiful and sunny, without too much smog. Everyone was enjoying the fellowship with one another by eating, playing games, swimming, and relaxing. It was just a perfect weekend.

Gary and I were sitting and chatting with friends when I heard Jacob yell. When I turned, I saw him running our way. He was shouting that something had bitten him on his foot. I could see it was red and swelling really quickly. We quickly checked his foot to ensure he'd not been bitten by a snake. We were concerned until we could see there were no punctures a snake bite would have shown. We knew what snake bites looked like; we had been sure to learn how to identify them since we did have rattlesnakes in the area. One had even visited us in our house one day by squeezing in from the garage into the house to stretch out along the shower in the downstairs bathroom, probably looking for a place to cool off. It was good that it wasn't a real big one, and with the proper snake catching gloves, we were able to get it out without anyone getting bit.

We were very relieved to see that a rattler had not bitten Jake, but the redness and swelling was not getting better. Still concerned, we left to take him to the closest emergency care center. He was examined pretty quickly after we arrived.

The doctor on duty said he didn't feel it was anything that some ice and medication wouldn't remedy, and if we noticed any different reactions or symptoms, call our doctor near home right away.

Then we returned to the lake to gather all our belongings we'd left in our haste for the emergency care. We shared what the doctor had said with concerned friends. By then the sun was setting, so everyone prepared to leave for home.

During the following weeks, no other symptoms were noticed from Jacob's bite. We continued our normal busy family routine, including school, church, sports, and all that most families with children balance each week. The only thing we did notice was he seemed to get worn out easier when playing soccer. He seemed to get sleepier earlier at night than before. He even had fallen asleep a few times when we had been out to eat dinner at a restaurant when we'd gone later than normal.

We had gone to a special place for dinner called The Big Yellow House. It was a special treat to go there; the restaurant was well-known for their delicious food. The original restaurant was actually a big yellow Victorian house that was turned into a restaurant. Then they started building Big Yellow House restaurants similar to the original around California to accommodate more people. All the new ones were decorated in a way that made you feel as if you were at grandma's house eating a good homestyle dinner. They were very welcoming and very comfortable. The food was so good that it was usually hard to get into one. Our family was excited about going there.

We'd gotten a table in one of the upstairs rooms in a corner with windows all around. It was perfect and turned out good for Jacob. He'd become so sleepy that night. Eventually, he quietly slipped from his chair and laid on the floor in the corner beside our table. We didn't feel so bad because he wasn't in anyone's way. Jacob had eaten most of his food but missed out on the delicious homemade desserts. We had tried to rouse him, but he was just too tired to wake up, even for dessert.

At first, we thought maybe he had just played extra hard outside on those days when he seemed extra tired, but in days to come, we became more concerned. When it was time for their next scheduled check-up, we discussed this with the doctor. After he finished the examinations, he hadn't seen anything to worry about; he found nothing medically wrong. He suggested maybe Jake might be losing interest in sports, or he might not be resting well because of a growth spurt he was going through. The doctor's news was good, but we were still concerned. It just all seemed so unusual for Jake.

We talked with Jake to ensure he wasn't just playing soccer because he knew how much his dad and I loved watching our kids play the game. If he didn't want to play any longer, we didn't want to make him feel like he had to because of us. He told us that wasn't it at all. He loved playing the game and being part of the team. "It just seems like I'm not able to keep up like I used to."

It was like his energy just seemed to leave him all of a sudden when he was running back and forth for some reason. The continuous running for ninety minutes in a game of soccer would have worn me out for sure, even when I was younger. But this was new for Jacob. He'd always been very active outside doing something until he'd come in for dinner or because it was getting dark. None of the kids sat in the house much at all. It was the time when kids were outside more than they were inside, like they seem to be doing nowadays. No hours were wasted on staring at video games and TVs. When asked if he wasn't sleeping well, he told us he was sleeping fine and always felt good and rested when he woke up in the mornings.

When visitors came from Ohio, we took them to all the California vacation sights. Jake would always seem to hang in there without getting worn out. We would spend long days for a week at a time never slowing down and trying to get them everywhere they wanted to go. Most of them could only come for a week each time, so they couldn't see everything in one trip. But they were able to return more times to see what they hadn't before, so we kept busy at first. I think you really need almost six months to get to see all there is in the whole state, if not longer. As you can see on a map, California is a very big state covering most of the west coast. It takes a lot of time to really see everything visitors want to visit from top to bottom.

We kept watching Jake to see if anything else seemed to change, as far as his health went. We never noticed anything different that indicated a problem. He seemed healthy, and we were all happy and felt we were right where we were supposed to be for many years to come. By this time, we had been living in California over eight years. But, as life goes, things can always change from what you think they will be, and when you are least expecting them, too.

"Jesus replied, 'You do not realize now what
I am doing, but later you will understand.'"
--John 13:7 (NIV)

Bundling up to go to top of the mountain to
play in the snow after just swimming in
the pool in Palm Springs.

CHAPTER 24: Never Say Never!

"I will instruct you and teach you in the way
you should go: I will counsel you with
My loving eye on you."
--Psalm 32:8 (NIV)

We had planned to remain right where we were at least until the kids were grown and graduated from high school. But it seemed this wasn't going to happen. Gary was contacted by another big air compressor company with an offer for him to join them. It would have been fine if we could remain right where we were, but if he decided to accept, we would leave California, and not only that, but they needed him to relocate to Ohio to work with their company there. Of all places! Really? Ohio?

As they say, *"Never say never!"* This was crazy having to move back to the cold Ohio winters, something we didn't have plans to ever do again. We would not be returning to the area from where we had come. But it wouldn't be too far from their either – just a little farther north, which meant the winter weather could be even colder. One good thing was we could get together with our family without having to drive a long time, so that would be nice for everyone. After so many years away, our family would enjoy being together for the holidays.

Facing the cold winters again was a big drawback for us. After becoming acclimated to the warm and sunny days of California for the past eight years plus, this was something we were not sure we wanted to give up, not to mention our friends and church family that we had grown to love. The kids had so many great friends, and there was a lot to consider when making this decision.

It seemed as if the new company really wanted Gary to join them. They began flying him to Ohio for meetings to discuss what his position would be, his pay, and benefits. The perks would help us sell our house in California and handle all the packing and moving and other expenses involved with a cross-country move.

They recommended we might consider having a new home built in West Chester, north of Cincinnati, going toward Dayton, Ohio. It was a growing area with many nice neighborhood developments with much to offer and a highly-rated school system.

If Gary did accept the offered position, he would need to travel back and forth until school was over because we knew we wanted the kids to finish the current school year. This decision was really hard to make; going back across the country seemed crazy. Getting settled where we were and being happy with things as they were now was not something we were prepared to consider leaving any time soon. Family came more than we had thought, so they were seeing how the kids had grown. We talked and talked, prayed, and prayed and in the end, we decided to return to Ohio. Even though I think we were all surprised we had made the decision to move, it just felt right for some reason.

Later, I made a trip to Ohio with Gary to see the town of West Chester and the surrounding areas. We found a new development we liked where we could build a house on a great lot with lots of beautiful trees all around. We talked with a builder there. It was in a good location, convenient to the school we wanted the kids to attend, and there were churches and shopping nearby. It was easy to get to the highway, so it would be more convenient for Gary to get to the Cincinnati or Dayton, Ohio, airports for business travel. With less traffic and congestion than in California and a choice of two different airports, this was a real plus when arranging flights.

We found we could have a nice brick home built without having to spend a lot of money, at least compared to California prices. The house would be better built and on a much larger lot, too. Even though we'd experience cold winters, the area would be beautiful with all the trees and surrounding nature. We felt good about deciding to move near family again, as well as old friends we'd grown up with. Even though our family and friends wouldn't have a *vacation home* in California any longer, I didn't doubt our family was happy about us coming home to Ohio.

After the current school year ended, our house sold quickly. The moving company packed our belongings and our new house was right on schedule. We'd be moving in when we arrived in Ohio. Everything was moving along like clockwork.

Over the weeks before school ended, we had visited and had been visited by friends to say our goodbyes, with hopes we'd be able to visit in the future.

After a few final goodbyes, we loaded into our van, along with Goldie, our Cocker Spaniel, and we began our cross-country trip to Ohio. We drove most of the day, stopped to sleep, then arose and drove more. Finally, after the tiring drive, we arrived in Ohio. While we awaited the moving van with our furniture and belongings, we visited with family.

With excitement, we moved into our new home, enrolled the kids in school, and registered the kids to play soccer. After being away so many years, it was good to be close to family and celebrate the holidays when they came to our house for Thanksgiving and Christmas. Then we met at different restaurants or at each other's homes for birthday celebrations. We shared many happy times and made great memories together.

We adjusted to the Ohio weather -- lots of rain, some tornados, and, of course, cold, wintery weather for months. The kids played soccer in the rain and cold, not having done that in California, but it didn't seem to bother them. It seemed, Gary and I were the only ones bothered by the weather, especially because we had to stand in the rain and cold to watch them! But regardless, it was always worth it, especially one cold, rainy day when Jason was running down the field toward the goal. He quickly glanced over to me and called out, "This one's for you Mom!" just as he kicked the ball toward the net. The ball shot past the goalie and in for a goal! Happy Birthday to me! I loved his gift!

We were thankful for the kids on their teams that Lori and the boys got to know. It had been harder to make new school friends because the houses were farther apart instead of close, as they had been in California. Students were bussed in from all over, eliminating the opportunity to visit each other's home as they had been doing in California. They only had a few friends with the kids living closer. It was good whenever they could visit and have outings with relatives and soccer friends.

Lori chose to try out and play on a semi-pro team. She didn't want to replace one of the girls who had played on the prior school team because she didn't feel that would be right and not a good way to make friends. Fortunately, she had a great experience playing with the semi-pro team. Even though Lori was the youngest player on the team, she did an outstanding job. It was always exciting to watch her, and the boys play soccer.

Gary began traveling during the week, and we had not attended the same church long enough to make good friends. But all in all, we were getting familiar with our surroundings and were enjoying how things were going. It really was a nice area to live.

After being back in Ohio for just a little while, we began to notice more and more that Gary's mother, Esther, seemed to have health problems. We arranged for her to come and stay with us for a while, so we could care for her and make her comfortable. As the weeks passed, Esther grew to need more and more assistance and medical care. Sadly, when we could no longer give her the care she needed, we were forced to make the heartbreaking decision to place her in a health-care facility.

We were recommended to a facility where she'd have a little efficiency apartment. A nurse would be available during different hours of the day for medical needs. If desired, dinners were prepared for the residents. As she was diabetic, it was necessary for her to have a proper diet and good dinners.

Visitation was allowed, and we could bring her home for the day when she felt okay. Unfortunately, she wasn't able to stay in this facility more than a few months. The administration felt she needed twenty-four hours-a-day care, which they were unable to provide for her.

As you can imagine, this was a hard time for our family, especially Gary. He had lost his father when he was young; now, it seemed he was facing the possibility of losing his mother sooner than we'd thought might happen. This was when we realized why this job had been offered to Gary – the timing of how everything had fallen in place. God had placed us here for Esther to make decisions for her she couldn't make herself. The diabetes, which is such an unpredictable disease, was causing her health to decline more rapidly. For years, she'd managed it well and had traveled to California for visits. Esther had been able to get around on her own without issues for quite a while. So, it was sad to see her needing lots of care and knowing it was hard for her not to be independent as she had been up until now. Gratefully, we were able to get her into a nursing home where Gary's cousin worked. It was a relief knowing his cousin would watch over her and ensure she had the best care possible. His cousin had lived with Esther while she attended nursing school in Cincinnati. Their closeness made it easier for Gary to move his mother into a permanent nursing home without feeling too guilty.

If we'd not decided to move back to Ohio and hadn't gotten help for Esther when she needed it most, we would never have forgiven ourselves. It would have been very difficult to know about her true needs if we'd stayed in California. Again, it affirmed that God knows what needs to be done and provides the way for it to happen at the exact time it is needed.

Our family visited Esther often; we received reports about her care and her condition regularly. It was comforting to know she was being well cared for. But it felt sad not to do more or have her with us.

Our move to Ohio had come quickly. Being with family again, assisting with Gary's mother's needs, adjusting to school changes, and making other adjustments seemed to be going by fast, even though it hadn't been a year. But what a year it had been thus far! And there would be more to come; hold on to your hat!

> *"The steadfast love of our Lord never ceases;*
> *His mercies never come to an end; they are*
> *new every morning; great is your faithfulness.*
> *'The Lord is my portion,' says my soul, 'there-*
> *fore I will hope in Him.'"*
> *--Lamentations 3:22-24 (ESV)*

CHAPTER 25: Here We Go Again

"When anxiety was great within me, your
consultation brought Joy to my soul."
--Psalm 94:19 (NIV)

When Gary came home a few weeks later and told me he had been asked to take a new position as the Western Regional Sales Manager for the company, I was thinking, *This cannot be happening,* especially after hearing where they needed him for this job. I bet you can guess! Yes! We would need to return to California. Unbelievable! And to top in all, the company management needed our move to take place as quickly as possible.

Needless to say, this news was unexpected. Occurrences within the company required the changes to be made hurriedly. They believed Gary was the best person for the job. There really wasn't much discussion about this move; it was more or less a *must do* situation in Gary's career. He and I made a quick trip flying out to find an existing house we could move into after making quick arrangements to get there.

We chose to go right back to Moreno Valley where we had left about a year ago to the day. We could have afforded to go to a *better* area of California now, but Moreno Valley had become an important part of our spiritual journey. The friends we all had made there had left a big void for us that we had come to realize. We also were pretty excited about going back to warm, sunny weather after being back for just one winter in Ohio. I think warm and sun won over cold and clouds.

Knowing Esther was getting the best possible care she could, and the fact Gary would be traveling back to Ohio frequently and could visit her helped remove any guilt feelings he had about moving back to California so quickly. This made me happy as I knew he struggled about being far away from her again.

It's amazing how quickly things can be accomplished when needed. A house bought, a house sold, a moving company packing up your belongings and loading them on the moving van, saying goodbye to family, driving back across country again, and returning to California before you know it. It all seemed like one long overnight dream: like we had never been gone. The only thing different was the house we were living in when we returned. It was a nice house, not as big as the one we had before, and we didn't have the great yard with the horses in the field behind it, but like everywhere, home prices had continued to rise, even in one short year, and we got into what we could quickly without having to wait for a new build. It was in a good neighborhood not far from the house we'd sold, so the kids attended the same schools. And with it closer to our church, we were happy with no complaints.

With the kids being older now, I decided to get a part time job during the hours they were in school. A new fabric store had opened just after we moved back, and I was excited to be able to work there and be surrounded by all the beautiful fabrics.

One of my hobbies was making quilts, and the more

fabric to choose from, the better. The best part of it all was I received great discounts by being employed there, so even though I usually spent most of my paycheck buying fabric, I was getting fantastic deals.

I was always telling Gary, "Look how much money I saved on all this beautiful fabric!"

He would always reply and still does, "You are spending money; how do you come to the conclusion you are saving money if you are spending it?" It is a running joke between us; I consider it saving; he considers it spending, and we agree to disagree, so no problem. I do have to confess though, that I still have a lot of that fabric I bought over 30 some years ago! So maybe I did go a little overboard!!

Later when Lori was old enough to work part time, she and one of her friends began working at the fabric store, too. They loved it and had fun working there as a first job. They had lots of funny stories about different things that happened when they were helping customers. It was a good experience for them as their first step into the working world. Lori never really enjoyed sewing much; however, she did make herself a skirt once, and that seemed to be enough for her. She had no desire to attempt making anything else. But she had fun, performed her job well, and that was good enough for me.

Life seemed to fall right back into the familiar routines as they were before. School and sports were again on track, and family and friends began coming for visits from Ohio again. I do think they were really happy we had moved back, so they had a place to stay when they wanted to come out West for a vacation, which was all good; we allowed them to explore on their own.

We had seen all the vacation spots so many times, we really had no desire to see them all again. They were fine with that and enjoyed their time out each day. They knew they had a comfortable place to return to each night to relax and be able to get a good night's sleep and rested up to explore again the next day.

The only thing I wish I could have had some control over was to slow down how fast the kids were growing up. Lori would be graduating from high school in just four short years. Then the boys would follow four years later. Being a Mommy was what was most important to me; I didn't like thinking they wouldn't be around before I was ready for that to happen. Of course, I never would be ready for an empty nest. I loved when they invited their friends home with them. They were always having such a good time together. Hearing their laughter was great. I hope their friends always felt welcome in our home. They were all good kids and never caused any real problems. I miss having them and their friends coming in and out, grabbing a bite to eat or something to drink, or just making me laugh. I never grew tired of it.

A couple of years after returning to California, Gary was out of town when he received the news his mother had passed away suddenly. He would go directly to Ohio, and I would follow as soon as I could make all the arrangements to get there. It was winter now; Ohio was cold and snowing. It was the kind of weather his mother didn't like. It was always hard for her to *get out and about* when she was healthier and able to drive, and she never looked forward to the cold winters when there was snow or ice on the roads. She had always been a busy lady, going places, helping others, and not driving when it snowed. She didn't drive until after Gary's father had died, so she still was pretty cautious about driving in inclement weather.

Gary made all the arrangements before I arrived in Ohio. Because of the weather, not a lot of people were able to attend the funeral. We knew they wanted to come and pay their respects. It was a sad time for us; standing at the gravesite with the wind and cold whipping around us and blowing the light snowfall seemed to add to the sadness even more.

We hadn't been there to hold her hand and weren't able to tell her how much we loved her just once more. We knew she had no doubt of our love, but you always wished you could say those words once more to your loved ones before they have departed this life. The wonderful thing was knowing she and Gary's father had loved the Lord; we could celebrate the knowledge and comfort she was in Heaven, and they were together again. It's a blessing knowing your family loves the Lord, and you will be reunited again for eternity is reason for celebrating even though they are greatly missed.

She was a special lady; she and Gary's family had taught me how to feel loved and show love for others. I will always be grateful to them for that. Lori was old enough to have spent a lot of time with her grandmother before we moved to California the first time; they shared a special closeness that Lori missed very much. Our daughter loved everything about her Grandma Esther and wanted to be just like her when she grew up. She continues saying that to this day, all the while smiling and laughing about memories of her. The boys were younger and didn't have the same chance to know her as well. They remember her always laughing and knowing she loved them.

All of her grandchildren loved her.

When we are around the other grandchildren, we have great time reminiscing about Grandma Esther and the good old days! She possessed a great smile with a tickled-sounding laugh we all cherish. Just looking at her picture recalls her laughter in our minds. Flying back to California was difficult, knowing that laugh was gone.

Please be kind to the elderly, always showing them the respect they deserve. One day you will experience the feeling of realization that your children have grown way too fast, and you will miss the times when they were little. This is the same feeling you get when the elderly are no longer with us. We miss talking to them again and just being in their presence.

When the elderly ramble on or repeat their stories, excuse the quirks you find annoying and just be a listening ear. It doesn't take much effort from you; be patient, so you won't regret not being there for them and / or being someone, they can talk to. Remember, if the Lord is willing, you will be old one day and might just desire more time with those you love.

"Stand up in the presence of the aged, show respect for the elderly and revere your God. I am the Lord."
--Leviticus 19:32 (NIV)

CHAPTER 26: 1989: What a Year it Was!

"But those who wait on the Lord shall renew
their strength; They shall mount up with wings
like eagles, they shall run and not grow wea-
ry, they shall walk and not faint."
--Isaiah 40:31 (NKJV)

We planned for 1989 to be a special time for our family. With Lori graduating from high school, we'd hoped to plan a great family vacation – perhaps to Hawaii to celebrate together and give her a special treat for graduation. She had accomplished hanging in there with all the moving and changes over the years and had managed to graduate with her classmates. The class of '89 would be the first graduating class from the new Canyon Springs High School. It had been built in the area after we'd returned from Ohio. The group of kids were close and had enjoyed their special years together; many shared a special bond. Some of the graduates are still good friends, staying in touch and sharing experiences, marriages, and children with each other regardless of living in different states.

After graduation, Lori wasn't certain what her plans were next. We didn't rush her to decide right away. We wanted her to enjoy some down time and have a fun summer without worrying about her future yet.

The boys would be starting eighth grade, but they would have a great summer of sports, friends, and family vacation. We eagerly anticipated summer fun. I knew the next four years would pass quickly, at least for me. Then the boys would be graduating, and I longed for as much time as I could get with all of us together. My wishes had always been to have twice as much time for each passing year when they were growing up. But time doesn't stop for anyone. Thankfully, I can recall some of those good memories.

It appeared we'd be permanent Californians as Gary's job was going great. He was helping to build the companies' business in this ever-growing state. It seemed a given there would be a continued need for air compressors. Along with his team, Gary had continued to keep the business growing and going well in the West.

Life was good, we were happy, and my only complaint was the terrible traffic and constant building everywhere. Houses were closer and closer; yards were smaller and smaller. We didn't travel to San Francisco or other far places as before. It took too long to get anywhere. But we had our children and friends close by, so all was good. Gary and I considered moving further inland to avoid crowding, but that would be in the future and just talk for now. We'd wait until after the boys graduated before looking at other areas.

This was our designated year for graduation and a family vacation. Ha! You know the quote, "The only constant in life is change." The expected graduation took place, but the exciting vacation to Hawaii would be replaced by a not so exciting trip in our motor home while driving back cross country; because Gary had been transferred to another state to help grow the business there! Really? We could be great cross country tour guides by now.

We were not traveling back to Ohio, and were happy about that, Gary's promotion this time was taking us to Charlotte, North Carolina. We were on our way to the South and a new experience. We'd only been back in California four years, never expecting this to happen again. I knew the kids were tired of moving back and forth; they had moved a lot compared to their friends and others. Their sense of stability was being shaken again.

Gary had flown back and forth to meet everyone, learn the job details, discuss the move, and plan his future there. The company had flown me there to look at areas where we might live. If we agreed to move in an existing house, our belongings would arrive before we did, allowing us to move right in. We were taken to dinners, met other employees and families, and went to a NASCAR race at the Charlotte Motor Speedway and sat in the company's skybox. I'd never been into NASCAR (sorry fans). Charlotte was a nice city – not too big and crowded – and easy to get around. The company was trying hard for Gary to accept the position. We didn't want to have a year there before returning to California as we'd once done. We weren't up to that scenario happening in the near future, we did want confirmation that that would not happen.

Gary and I liked an area twenty miles north of Charlotte with a huge, beautiful lake – Lake Norman – with surrounding gorgeous trees. There were boat ramps, marinas, and restaurants where you could enjoy a meal looking out of the vastness of water, the calmness of sailboats, and the speed boats. The surrounding towns were quaint and charming, a nice change from hustle and bustle of California. To travel twenty miles in California took forty-five minutes or more, whereas traveling twenty miles in Charlotte took fifteen minutes. In California, we fought congestion, bumper to bumper traffic, and if an accident happened, you could sit still in one place half the day, waiting for everything to get cleared away. Charlotte was beginning to look better and better to us.

We knew we'd be able to find a church from the many we saw in the area. The area would be growing as it was in every part of the country, but this had more of a small-town atmosphere, which was appealing. We wanted to slow down, stop, and smell the roses rather than constantly rushing about. We could stop and appreciate nature's beauty. Charlotte was a quick trip where there were Uptown restaurants, theater, museums, and other outings. People were friendly everywhere we went, taking time to talk with us and make us feel that they were genuinely happy to meet us. North Carolina was definitely pulling all the right strings.

"The righteous keep moving forward, and those with clean hands become stronger and stronger."
--Job 17:9 (NLT)

CHAPTER 27: Decisions, Decisions

"Let your eyes look straight ahead; fix your
gaze directly before you. Give careful thought
to the paths for your feet and be steadfast
in all your ways."
--Proverbs 4:25 (NIV)

After returning home, we shared with the kids what we'd seen and learned, and even though it was hard, we explained we'd made the decision to move from California to North Carolina. It had been more of a struggle to decide as the kids were older, and we needed to consider the changes in their lives. They'd expected their futures to be in California. It had taken a lot of thought and prayer. Our trust in God led us to make this decision – an unexpected move to North Carolina. One day, we'd learn the reason for all of this just as we'd learned about our previous unexpected moves.

This move would be the hardest for Lori. At a critical time in her young life, everything was changing. It probably felt as if a high wall had been built around her, and she couldn't see a way to get over it to the other side. Even though she didn't have post-graduate plans, she had never considered having to plan anywhere but where she'd called home most of her life and without the support of good friends. I felt bad to see her upset and sad.

The boys had been planning to play soccer in high school with their teammates whom they'd played with for years. This was disappointing, but they were confident they'd make new school friends and soccer friends. Sports allowed them to meet other players and make new friends quickly. We didn't worry as much about their adjustments.

This would be a big change for all of us; moving from what had been familiar for so many years would be a hard adjustment. It seemed we'd had to do it too often for Lori to handle. I thought moving around and seeing more of the world was exciting, but Lori didn't feel the same.

"When I get married one day, I'm going to stay in the same place forever. I don't like picking up and moving around." And true to herself, she has moved to different houses but has remained in the same general area since moving to North Carolina.

My dad was very happy about our decision to move, as he'd never been thrilled with us living in California because of all the earthquakes we experienced while living there. He enjoyed visiting us but didn't stay long for fear of getting caught in an earthquake during his visit. It wasn't like he had not experienced bad weather. As a Merchant Marine during World War II there were many violent storms on the ocean during his time of service. Also, living in Ohio we experienced blizzards and tornados, which were some pretty harsh conditions to be in. Plus, he was a volunteer fireman in our town, so he experienced and witnessed many disasters, but for some reason, he feared being where an earthquake might happen and didn't like us being there either.

When you live in California, it can become a bad habit

to become used to earthquakes that you really don't take them to seriously, especially if you haven't experienced any real damage or injuries. We'd been blessed by being kept safe and not having a horrible experience when they did occur. There really is no preparing for a potential earthquake like warnings for tornados or hurricanes. There is no predicting what might happen. Severity is only known after the earthquake. Instruments gather information about magnitude, intensity, and duration of earthquakes while the quake is happening and during aftershocks, which can continue for weeks at a time. All over the world, quakes happen and can cause a little shaking with no damage or mass destruction.

If the magnitude was an eight or nine or higher, we knew what could happen. Thankfully, where the fault ruptured and proceeded along the fault lines that ran near us were never close enough to cause real destruction to our home or property. I don't remember any warnings for earthquakes; maybe there is some type of guidance for preparation in areas where earthquakes are more likely to happen. It wasn't good for us to become lax and casual about the possibility one could occur anytime without warning.

We didn't experience many earthquakes and when we did, they were milder in our area, although we did have a few strong ones that caused hard jolting and shaking. They did give us cause for fear, but we were very relieved and thankful when they were over and everyone was okay.

One particular earthquake seemed like it was never going to quit shaking and jerking us around. It occurred during the middle of the night. We woke up right away when it first started happening. We heard Lori calling and knew she was panicking. Her bedroom was downstairs; ours and the boys' bedrooms were upstairs. She ran to the bottom of the stairs when the rumbling and shaking started and tried to climb up the stairs. Lori was so scared. Each time she tried to climb the stairs, jerking and shaking caused her to fall backwards. We were tumbling, too, and couldn't grab her hand before another jolt would part us again. Finally, after several attempts, we all managed to make it together and were able to comfort her and the boys until it all stopped.

Hanging plants and lights were swinging; small items throughout the house were falling from shelves and counters. Amazingly, there was no real damage. We were safe except for a few bruises. It's pretty frightening to feel so helpless and unable to do anything about what is happening around you, especially when it is one of the first strong earthquakes you experience.

An earthquake we especially remember was a different type that caused more of a rolling effect instead of shaking and jolting action. It occurred in the middle of the night, too. When Gary and I awoke from hearing the rumble and tried to get up to check on the kids, we were not able to walk without being off balance and stumbling around. Trying to climb up or descend stairs was almost impossible. It was like trying to stand on rolling logs moving down a flowing river. Lori and Jacob had awakened and were where we could see them and know they were safe. Jason, however, hadn't come out of his room and didn't answer when we called him. Struggling, we made our way to his room and worried something may have knocked him out or maybe he had fallen and landed hard and was unconscious.

At the time, Gary and I never liked their choice of beds. Waterbeds were the popular thing all kids wanted, so we'd given in and bought each one a waterbed. When we finally reached Jason's room and looked in, he was still lying on his bed, appearing to be sound asleep. He was just riding the waves of his waterbed, rolling back and forth like a rocking cradle. Maybe he was dreaming about lying on a float in the ocean or swimming pool. Seeing he was all right, we had to laugh from relief and from the scene in front of us. Jason still didn't stir from his sleep, so we just allowed him to be while the rest of us stayed together until the rolling finally stopped.

The next morning, we asked him if he felt the earthquake at all, and he just gave us this look like we were pulling his leg and joking around with him. He had never been aware, not even for one minute, that we had a pretty severe earthquake through the night. He was a little disappointed that he hadn't got to feel how fun it must have been laying on the waterbed rolling him back and forth like being on big wave.

At any rate, Dad was relieved about our days of California earthquakes coming to an end. There have been some minor ones in the Carolinas but nothing like those again. One afternoon when friends and I were in the movie theater in Mooresville, North Carolina, a mild earthquake occurred. I noticed right away my friends looked terrified while I sat there as if nothing were happening. Without thinking I said, "It's just an earthquake," which wasn't very thoughtful of me. They had never felt one before. Instead of acting like it wasn't a big deal, I should have been reassuring. Fortunately, it didn't last long and our focus returned to the movie. Authorities measured it as a magnitude three or four. Because of its rarity, it was the talk of the town for quite a while.

> *"The name of the Lord is a strong tower; the righteous run to it and are safe."*
> *--Proverbs 18:10 (NKJV)*

CHAPTER 28: Cross Country Drive / Sad to Happy Moments

"For He will command His angels concerning
you to guard you in all your ways."
--Psalm 91:11 (NIV)

Leaving California seemed a bit melancholy. The drive cross country seemed to drag on, especially because our daughter was very sad and stayed cocooned in her bunk, the overhead compartment over the cab of the motorhome. Lori wasn't interested in the discoveries we pointed out along the way. Gary and I tried to get her mind off friends and engage with us, but it wasn't working. The first couple of days were especially hard. We tried to make it fun for the kids in hopes of cheering her. The boys were really trying to show interest and were concerned about their sister, too. They were not used to seeing her so sad and crying and sleeping so much. As a parent, it hurts when you can't make things better for your child no matter what you do. She just needed time.

When the kids were younger, we'd taken a trip to the Grand Canyon. Lori wasn't happy about being there then and was like a mother hen, sticking close to her brothers. She feared one of them would get too close to the edge and slip and fall to the bottom. That would have been a serious injury or even death.

"I will never come back here. When I have kids some-day, I will never let them come here, no matter what!" Unfor-tunately, her fear disallowed her joy in the awesomeness and surrounding beauty.

Gary took a picture of Lori, the boys, and me standing at the edge of the Canyon on a very safe spot where you can see the depth and vastness of the Canyon in the background. He wanted to show the beautiful colored layers of rock lower toward the bottom. Lori wasn't happy, but she stood with us. It's obvious from the photo she wasn't happy.

Because we were driving near the area again, we decid-ed to go there and take another picture in the exact location as earlier as they were older and experiencing the same vis-it. I should have known better, but we decided to ask in case she'd changed her mind about her previous statement years before.

Lori adamantly said, "No!" There wasn't a chance of getting her out of the motorhome for another picture, so we just passed by, never mentioning the idea again. To this day Lori still says she will never return to the Grand Canyon.

Fortunately, we witnessed beautiful sights, which was an education in itself. We visited historical sights and expe-rienced the changes of geographical features in the different regions of the country. Our boys really enjoyed these experi-ences and being outside to explore when we stopped at camp-grounds. All and all, it was a good trip without incident, vehi-cle problems, sickness, or injuries. And we were thankful. Lori joined us in visiting some of the places and tried her best to seem interested as the days went by.

After a side trip to Surfside Beach in South Carolina

to visit Gary's sister and husband, Helen and Clay, who lived there, we continued to Charlotte and checked in a hotel close to Gary's new office on Tyvola Road. During the two days we were there, the kids enjoyed being out of the RV and having space to spread out and a big pool to swim in whenever they wanted.

There was lots of available food whenever they wanted it. I admit it was nice not to be in such tight quarters. While we waited for the moving van, Gary found his new position pleasing and I caught up on laundry.

Finally, our furnishings and clothes arrived. We were happy to move into our new home in Cornelius, North Carolina. It was a spacious home with a view of Lake Norman across the street and a vacant lot there where we could go swimming and dock a boat – just a few steps away. The kids were excited, and the boys liked being able to fish off the dock or in a boat. It was a great relief to witness their excitement, which had been the same as Gary's and mine the first time we visited.

The house was surrounded by big, beautiful trees everywhere we looked. Big trees were something we didn't have in our yards in California. Most homes had very small yards and small trees, unlike the Carolinas. These were climbing trees, which thrilled the boys. And having the lake outside our door was exciting.

Lake Norman is a man-made lake that was created between 1959 and 1963 by Duke Power Company. They had set off a charge of dynamite in 1959 to start clearing the area to create a lake that would end up covering 32,500 acres with surface water and have 520 miles of shoreline and about 50 square miles of land. Many of the farmlands were purchased by Duke Power and they flooded houses, barns, farm equipment, roads and more. Locals share their experiences as they watched the lake rising and covering their land. There are fascinating stories to read about or hear about during those years of preparing and filling the area with water. I recommend you read one of many books written about Lake Norman.

In 1989, this was a quiet and peaceful lake to spend a relaxing day boating, fishing, or skiing. Most homes scattered along the shoreline were small or vacation cottages. Fishing was great and the lake, a real gem, was considered out in the country. No one really thought about living there full time if they worked in Charlotte. We spent many hours on the lake and built a new home in Mooresville on a beautiful lake front lot years later.

The boom happened there also, and you began seeing more and more houses built on the shores all around the lake, and unfortunately more and more traffic also. We would eventually sell our home in 2020 and move into a home in South Carolina, where it seemed we spent more time than not after we had gotten a condo there. The lake was wonderful, but the beach seemed to be calling our names. I do miss the magnificent, spectacular sunsets on Lake Norman. I could view them from the back of the house – whether looking out of a window or sitting on the back porch. There were brilliant colors and clouds, making artistic movements, mingling with the amazing colors.

Sunsets are my thing – whether there were clear days or stormy skies. For me, sunsets and sunrises display the artwork of God better than anything else. They are never the same, so you can always find me running for my phone or camera many mornings and evenings to capture a shot of their magnificence. Sometimes when I see the shades of oranges, purples, blues, and yellows, it's as if it is the first time I've experienced them. They are always an amazement – a surprise -- because they are so unique. To me, sunsets are reminders to be thankful for each day I am given and a hope for the morning when I might have the opportunity to be greeted with God's beautiful sunrise once again. These are spiritual connections for me, reminding me to praise God for all His goodness and glory. Sunsets and sunrises are just a glimpse of what we have to look forward to in Heaven when our days on this earth are finished.

"The Heavens declare the glory of God,
the skies proclaim the work of His hands."
--Psalm: 19-1 (NIV)

CHAPTER 29: A New Home;
A New Experience

"I have said these things to you, that in me you
may have peace. In the world you will have
tribulation, but take heart, I have overcome
the world."
--Isaiah 41:10 (ESV)

After settling in, the boys enjoyed fishing and climbing. I heard them out back having a great time, but when I looked out, I couldn't see them. Puzzled, they had noticed me looking for them. One of the boys called, "Mom. Look up!" When I did, I caught my breath. They were sitting in the tip top of a giant pine tree, swaying back and forth. *Oh my gosh! Those branches are not strong enough to hold my two teenage boys much longer. At any minute, those branches are going to snap, and I'll see them falling to the hard ground. I'll have to rush them to a hospital.* Then I remembered I didn't have a clue where a hospital was. I held my breath once again as they started their way down. Finally, they made it down – slowly and safely – and no broken bones.

We talked about the skinny trees, and they admitted how scary it was up there and how difficult it was to come down because it was hard to find a sturdy limb to stand on. They happily received my advice about climbing big, strong-limbed trees from now on, as well as not trying to get to the very tip top. I felt better. I didn't want to squash their fun by carrying on like a maniac Mom! Besides, the tomboy in me re-membered how much fun I always had climbing trees. I knew they loved being up high, looking out as far as they could see.

The big trees all around had been a deciding factor for us. After all, it was more humid here than in the West, so shade would be appreciated as we sat on our deck and porch. It was relaxing to sit and watch the birds flying in and out of the trees and watching them build nests to lay their eggs. We didn't have many birds flying around in our yards in Califor-nia, so I was ready to get bird feeders and watch the different kinds of birds feasting on the seeds we provided.

There was just so much to appreciate here when being outside. The Carolina blue skies, the beauty of the waters of the lake, the lack of smog, and being able to hear the sounds of nature all around us made it special.

Even though Lori was trying to adjust, she was feeling lost and alone without her good friends to spend time with and talk to each day. She was really missing them. It had been such an abrupt and unexpected change for her to get used to. She didn't know the area or where she could get a job or plan for further education. This made her miss her friends more than ever.

From the travel points Gary had earned from all his traveling, we got Lori a ticket, so she could go and visit her friends for a week or two. We hoped they could spend time sharing all the emotions and feelings they had about the changes that had occurred. None of them were expecting this move to happen in their young lives. We hoped a visit would help her decide what she wanted to do next as far as working or going to college.

Lori had been a big help unpacking and sorting when we moved in. Her room was in order, so maybe a trip back would give her the opportunity to say a proper goodbye that would help her accept the change and make her future in North Carolina to become an enjoyable experience. She was happy about the trip. It was good to see her excited instead of sad. We just hoped and prayed she would want to come back and not decide to stay there permanently.

We had always been a close-knit family since we had moved from extended family when the kids were so young; the five of us were a real team. I did feel Lori would come back, but you never know what your children might feel when they are far away from you and with good friends again. Lori and I had always had a close mother – daughter relationship (and we still do). And she has always been Daddy's Little Girl. Neither Gary nor I were ready for her to be far away from us forever, but I didn't want her to be miserable either. Only time would tell what she'd decide.

The trip to California actually turned out to be a good thing. We'd been in the house a little over two weeks when we took her to the airport for her flight. That same evening, the weatherman reported about a storm possibly developing into a hurricane as it gained strength crossing the Atlantic Ocean. On September 9, 1989, reports stated a cluster of thunderstorms that had begun off the coast of Africa had now become a tropical depression southeast of the Cape Verde Islands. By September 13, it had become a hurricane, turning west-northwest and causing it to slow and weaken some as it moved across the water. On September 17, just past midnight, Hurricane Hugo struck Guadeloupe. The eye moved over St. Croix early on the eighteenth and had accelerated. It appeared to be moving at slow speed toward Puerto Rico and the U.S. Virgin Islands.

The weatherman warned we should expect some wind and rain but hurricanes usually didn't come as far inland as Charlotte. We received no warning statements advising residents to prepare for hurricane force winds, tornados, or flooding. Nothing suggested we prepare for power outages or have bottled water on hand. Therefore, we felt safe from any type of destruction as we were three hundred plus miles inland from the ocean. We checked the weather report off and on for updates to ensure there were no drastic changes to worry about. Hurricanes were all new to us.

We went out to purchase groceries and other things we needed that we hadn't picked up yet since moving into the house. No one seemed concerned about the weather report, so that made us feel better about it all. We still needed to get our North Carolina driver's licenses, car tags, and to ensure we had everything the boys needed for the school year and for soccer. These tasks were our main focus at the time. Thus far, the day was fine.

After moving into the house, we'd gotten our two dogs out of the kennel, they had been flown here ahead of us. They were finally settled into our new home. They loved having a big yard to run around in; and we moved them into the garage at night with big beds they seemed to enjoy sleeping in. The cats (which are always in charge) and had traveled here with us in the motor home, slept wherever they chose to.

We continued watching the weather reports for updates on the hurricane. There were still no warnings to be prepared for anything worse than some wind and rain that might come our way, but no one expected any problems in our area. We planned to find a place for storing our RV in the next couple of days. We also planned to drive around and get acclimated to the area and locations, i.e., locating the closest hospital, driving to the school the boys would attend, getting them registered, and going to the Department of Motor Vehicles to get our North Carolina driver's license and car tags. We were busy most of the day running these errands and getting things on our to do list done.

Later forecasts reported Hurricane Hugo had caused damage to the U.S. Virgin Islands, and as it kept moving, it was upgraded to a category five hurricane. It was moving at a fast speed through the middle of the Atlantic and was now nearing Puerto Rico. It would change speed as it came toward the different islands.

On September 19, the hurricane had now turned and was picking up speed. The path it was taking looked like it might be heading somewhere along the east coast of the United States. They were hoping when and where it made landfall, it would cause the hurricane to turn and head back out to sea instead of coming inland.

Then, on September 20, a more concerning report came to our attention. Hugo seemed to be on a steady course heading right toward South Carolina. Now we were very alert and began to pay more attention to the reports. We were getting worried about Gary's sister and husband. They were only a block from the beach, and if the winds and rains were as strong as they were reporting, they would be flooded for sure, and there might even be a chance their house could end up with lots of damage or even be destroyed from the wind and ocean surges that were expected.

We called them and told them to come to North Carolina and stay with us in case it got too dangerous there. They told us they were preparing to evacuate and decided that they would go inland to Florence, South Carolina, which was some seventy miles from the coast. They felt they would be safe there. They did not want to come all the way to our house because they wanted to be able to get right back to check on their house as soon as they were allowed to return to their area. If they were as far inland as we were, the traffic would be even worse to get back, and they didn't want to take the chance of getting stuck in traffic and not be able to get back quickly to check on things.

We understood and asked them to please keep in touch and to keep us updated as to how they were. Once this was over, we volunteered to help them with clean up and promised to get there as soon as possible. We said goodbye and they headed for a hotel to check in.

It was September 21, which happened to be my forty-first birthday. We were glued to the television and prayed Gary's sister and her family would be safe where they had gone. Instead of going out for my birthday dinner like we had planned, we sat and watched hoping to hear Florence wasn't getting any damaging weather. Gary and I wanted to know Helen and Clay were safe.

The weather report was now being aired without taking a break; the TV stations continued reporting the path and what was happening along the way. They now predicted the hurricane would make landfall through the night, but it depended on the path and speed changes to know exactly where and when it might make actual landfall.

Along with most other people in Charlotte and the surrounding area, we'd retired to bed still feeling we would be safe. None of us heard the report at midnight; Hurricane Hugo had picked up strength, becoming a category five again with winds up to 140 m.p.h. and was headed right toward the Charleston, South Carolina, area. It made landfall, touching down on Sullivan's Island and The Isle of Palms before anyone was prepared. This area was only about a ten-minute drive across the bridge over the Charleston Bay into Charleston.

Even more unfortunate for us in the Charlotte area, who were sound asleep at this time, we had no knowledge that instead of Hugo turning back out toward the ocean after making landfall as the forecasters expected to happen, it continued moving inland. It passed by Columbia, South Carolina, and seemed to follow I-77 up to Charlotte, North Carolina. About five hours after it had made landfall near Charleston, we were awakened by the strong forces of wind, rain, and loud noises. It sounded as if a freight train was speeding past our house and through our back yard.

We had not been prepared at all for this nightmare. No one had. Everything went black as far as you could see. We could hear the cracking and crashing down of trees, and the telephone and electric poles were falling, as well. We heard and saw the explosions of transformers up and down the streets. We were very scared and really didn't know what to do. With no electricity we were not able to see anymore reports on TV or even turn on a radio. All systems were down, and the phones were dead. Our home had a well for our fresh water, but the electric pump didn't work without electricity, so we could not even make coffee or get a drink of water.

The only thing we could do was wait for the morning light, so we could see to get around better and be able to figure out what was damaged and what needed to be done. It was more frightening than we had ever been during an earthquake. I was thankful Lori was safe in California and not here. The boys, yes, even Jason, had heard it and came running to see what was happening. We really didn't know what to tell them; except to pray we would be safe.

The wind continued to howl, and the rain pelted so hard it sounded like it could come through the roof at any minute. We made our way to the garage door to let the dogs in with us, so they wouldn't be scared any longer. We knew they had been very scared from all the loud noises happening. They weren't used to thunderstorms, let alone hurricanes. Seldom did we experience thunderstorms in Southern California. When the dogs managed to calm down, the boys cuddled up with them and comforted each other through it all, which was good.

Now, Gary and I were really worried about Helen and Clay, but there was no way to get in touch with anyone who would know the situation in Florence near the hotel where they had gone. We knew being seventy miles inland was not good news. If we were getting this much damage here, it had to be really bad where they were. We prayed they were all safe and their house was not completely destroyed.

Our family in Ohio would be concerned about us as soon as they saw the news about the hurricane coming inland to Charlotte and continuing north through Cornelius where we lived. Also, Lori would be frantic when she awoke and heard what had happened. Of course, she would try to call right away. When she couldn't get in touch with us and hear our voice, we knew it would really be hard for her, she would fall apart not knowing if we were safe or hurt in some way. I was thankful she wasn't alone and had her friends and their families to comfort her. There was just no way to let anyone know we were safe.

"Our soul waits for the Lord; He is our
help and our shield."
--Psalm 33:20 (NKJV)

CHAPTER 30: Awaking to a Disaster

"We are hard pressed on every side, but not
crushed; perplexed, but not in despair;
persecuted, but not abandoned; struck down,
but not destroyed."
--2 Corinthians 4: 8-9 (NIV)

When it began to get lighter outside, we could see fallen trees everywhere in our backyard. Some were still falling, appearing as if they were moving in slow motion as the final roots, trying to hang on, began to lose strength and finally pull away from the ground. It made me sad watching them fall; I felt like a little bit of my strength was eroding away each time one fell. Utility poles had been broken, thrown this way and that way across the roads and yards. Wires were drooping and strewn everywhere. Up and down the street as far as we could see, there were many houses with fallen trees on their roofs. One house was completely covered by trees. It was one of the houses that had been there before the lake was actually filled, and it had been saved from being buried beneath the water when they were filling the lake.

The house sat on a higher elevation, and our road curved toward it and ended at that house. You would have driven right off the lot into the lake if you tried to go any farther past it. It sat on a point lot that jetted out into the lake and the road must have gone downhill from that point before the lake had been filled. It was one of the few remaining cabin-type, round-shaped structures left around the lake. Although we had not yet met the owner, we were told an elderly lady lived there alone. I prayed hard she was not hurt or suffering in any way. I knew as soon as anyone could get out and safely walk around without any danger, they would first check on her to ensure she was alright.

When it was finally light enough to go out and safely walk around, we saw trees down everywhere in the back yard and some in the front yard. We walked to the side of our house and were amazed to see trees that had fallen toward our yard from the lot next door. All the tall pines the boys had climbed to the top of had fallen into the yard straight as the wind had blown them, except for the ones that were straight across from the house. Instead of falling straight and landing on the house, they had fallen at an angle.

Each of the trees, which could have hit the house looked as if they had been carefully placed in a scattered pattern from the others. They had landed as if guided to ensure they would miss the house and had been laid on either side of the house so they would not crash through the roof or walls of the house. It could be imagined that great long, strong arms had reached down and spread them on each side of the house. There was only one single pine tree that had grazed a part of the front porch roof, damaging only one corner of it and breaking a support pole and part of the railing around the porch. That was the only destruction to our house. We were sad so many trees had been broken or fallen in our yard, but that was nothing to be upset about when our house did not suffer any trees crashing through the roof and leaving our home open to all the wind and rain pouring that could have flooded the inside. Even the RV hadn't received any real damage while sitting on the side of the road. There were just some dings here and there.

Our mess was just a matter of cleaning up the yard and making minimum repairs to the porch and split rail fence around the backyard. There was no doubt in our minds that we had been protected all through this unexpected disaster, which had traveled this far inland, something a hurricane had never done before through this area.

Everyone was relieved and very thankful the elderly lady in the round house was safe and uninjured. She was just badly shaken as anyone would have been. Some of the men had cleared a path to get to her door and check on her. Everyone would be watching over her to ensure she had what she needed and wouldn't be afraid until family could arrive to help and be with her.

Almost immediately neighbors checked on neighbors and found no one injured. We began hearing the sound of chain saws starting up all over the area. The fallen trees were being cut to make paths through the roads, so vehicles could get around. The roaring sound of the chain saws were heard from morning to night for months all over the South. It became a constant noise that stayed in your head even after they were quiet each evening. We didn't have one; there wasn't a need for us to have one in California, so we would have to wait to cut the trees in our yard later when we could purchase one. We just got busy cleaning up the smaller branches and the debris all around us.

We weren't aware until later that my dad had seen the news, gone out and bought some chain saws and had loaded them in his truck. As soon as he could get through and get to our home, he would drive from Ohio. We were surprised and very thankful when he pulled up in our driveway a few days later with the chainsaws and other tools in his truck. He was ready to get working to help us. He knew we didn't have a chain saw and also knew it would be hard to find one around here to purchase when stores did reopen. People would be waiting in a line to buy them as quickly as they could, and by the time we could even drive to where there was a store selling them, they would already be sold out. We had never been so excited about chain saws before when Dad pulled them out of his truck.

After just a short rest from his long drive, Dad, Gary, and the boys got busy cutting trees. It would have taken us forever to get all that work done if he had not arrived with all we needed. He was always a hardworking man and continued doing what he could for others until the very end of his life. He helped not only his family, but many others as well -- anyone with a need that he knew about.

There were many businesses that were unable to open because of no electricity but had signs posted saying they had hoses hooked up and water was available, free of charge, so those of us who didn't have drinking water could take containers to fill up. The owners of a favorite local family-owned breakfast restaurant that had been in the area for years, spread the word they had a generator going and were brewing hot coffee, available for all to come by and get in the mornings for as long as they had coffee to make.

The little restaurant was called *Bacon and Eggs* and everyone in the area would stand in line to wait and eat breakfast when it opened. It was always the best breakfast you could eat and always cooked exactly as you liked. We were all very sad in later years when the area had grown and it was sold and torn down to be replaced with a McDonalds. That spot just didn't seem right without the old *Bacon and Eggs* sitting there. Progress always seems to take away too many of the great places many people enjoy and miss.

Hurricane Hugo was the strongest hurricane to make landfall on the continental United States in the previous two decades at that time produced some of the highest storm tide heights ever recorded along the East Coast. The wind and rain from Hugo caused tremendous destruction to an area that virtually had never seen such impacts from a tropical storm system like this before. Again, we had been spared from the destruction we saw all around us. God has always been so good to us.

Today, you can search and find many reports on the Internet, which show all the destruction left from Hugo. You can see the total path it had traveled through the United States after it made landfall near Charleston and continued through the different states up to Canada where they felt some of the effects from the wind and rain before it was finally gone off the weather map for good.

In Charlotte and the surrounding areas alone, it was reported that more than eighty thousand trees had fallen, some that had been growing for close to one hundred years. More than 700,000 residents were without power for weeks. Many schools and businesses were closed even longer until they could get power again. States from all over sent crews to come and help restore the mass power outages all over the South.

Our family managed just fine. We weren't about to complain when at least we had a nice dry house to be in and able to sleep in our own beds each night. You quickly learn how to do things differently when you have to. I did have to wonder now though if my dad was going to suggest that maybe we shouldn't live here now, but he didn't, and I was sure not going to bring it up. He just kept working hard to help us in any way he could, getting things cleared and fixed. Everyone was working together to help each other any way possible.

We had the opportunity to meet most of our neighbors during this time, and we knew we all could count on each other whenever we needed something from then on. It certainly was not the best of circumstances to meet each other, but we all became close and shared a real connection from then on. It is wonderful how everyone comes together when there is a disaster; I do not mean to discount that at all, not by any means, but it would be even more wonderful if that was the way we were all the time with each other, not just during a disaster. It seems the world is just too complicated and evil to accomplish that, but we can at least share a smile or kind word with others we come in contact with each day. That is better than nothing at all. Be sure to do that when you have the opportunity and be part of making the world a better place, showing more love instead of hate that sadly seems to have become the normal emotion these days.

*"Let Love be genuine. Abhor what is evil;
hold fast to what is good."*
---*Romans 12:9 (ESV)*

Cleaning part of the yard after
Hurricane Hugo hit in September 1989.

CHAPTER 31: Lessons Learned/ So Thankful

"Devote yourselves to prayer, being
watchful and thankful."
--Colossians 4:2 (NIV)

We all learned a very important lesson from all that had happened during our experience with Hurricane Hugo. From that point on, we were going to have certain necessities stocked up and be prepared when we heard about a possible hurricane moving across the Atlantic toward the East Coast. We now fill up the bathtub or any other vessel that can hold lots of water. This way we will have water to take a sponge bath and can use buckets full of water to flush the toilets. The water can also be boiled on a grill to make instant coffee, instant grits, or oatmeal and other things like that to eat if we are without electricity.

We now have hand-turning can openers and get food that we can just eat from the can if we can't cook something on the grill or just don't feel like cooking! We make sure to do this even if there is a small chance of a hurricane coming our way. If we are told to evacuate, we don't ignore the warning. We take it seriously and pack up and get out of town as soon as we can.

Living where we do now, close to the coast, we can more

than likely be guaranteed to experience hurricanes every year. Some might not be as threatening, and we can stay, but if they are reported to involve very high winds and rains, it is best to go if told to. It isn't fun being away from your home and belongings, wondering what is happening and when you will be able to go back, but it is better than someone being injured or killed by taking a chance and staying.

We learned a few months later what was necessary to do here in the South when there happened to be a little snow coming down out of the sky, too. When the first snow began to fall after we moved here, we noticed that everyone seemed to be rushing to the grocery store, almost in a panic. We could not figure out what was going on, but I had needed a few things from the grocery, so I wandered out later to pick up some things.

What a surprise I was in for when I got there. When I went to the bread aisle, all the bread was gone; the shelves were stripped bare! Then after doing some more shopping, I went to the aisle that normally contained the milk. It too was bare. I could not figure out what was going on. I began to listen in on conversations and learned that because of the little bit of snow coming down, everyone rushed out to get bread and milk in case they were not able to get out if it continued to snow for a while. I was amazed; there was only a dusting of snow out there. Had I missed something about a blizzard coming? I had not missed anything. The snow that was forecasted was just the little snow that had come, and that was all there was going to be. We learned that at the very first snowflake here, everyone thought it was necessary to get out there and get the bread and milk because they weren't used to driving in any amount of snow, not even a snowflake apparently.

Growing up in Ohio and having blizzards made it seem so funny to us that our neighbors panicked when just a little snow was forecasted. It must have been what all Southerners were taught to do. Get out there and get that bread and milk. Clean out all of it just in case it snows more than they say it is going to. *So silly,* we thought at the time. Of course, now, after being here over thirty-three years, we seem to get out there and grab our bread and milk right along with everyone else. I guess we can be considered real Southerners now!

We were happy for Lori that she had been out in California during the hurricane and so thankful she had not been flying back home when it all was happening. I knew she was beside herself with worry not being able to get in touch with us. I hoped she realized that it was because all the systems were down and not because something had happened to us. It was a while before we could get in touch with her and other family members to let them know we were safe and not injured.

Lori did return to North Carolina as soon as she could after that, and we were so happy she did. I guess her not being able to get in touch with us had made her really miss us all. She did not want to be so far away again in case there was another situation like this. She has never returned to California since that time. Also, the boys have never really had any desire to go back and see their friends again. They all learned to love living in North Carolina, we all did. It is nice now for us to be close enough to travel back up there and visit family and friends, or them come here to South Carolina to see us without it being a long drive.

After Lori returned home, she shared with us what it

was like for her not knowing if we were okay during the hurricane for so long. She said when someone had finally turned on the TV the following day and saw the news about Hugo and the destruction it had caused and where, she had immediately tried to call and get in touch with us. Of course, she, nor any of our other relatives or friends had been able to get through for some time with all the lines down all over the area. She said she had been so scared and was crying almost in hysterics not knowing what had happened; if we were okay and if our house was still standing.

Her friends were trying to comfort her. She said they thought if they could make her laugh it would help her to stop crying and calm down some, but being teenagers, they weren't really sure what to do. She said they went and got a big fan and set it in front of her, turning in on full blast and then sprayed water through the back so it came out on her blowing with the wind saying, "This is probably what it feels like for your parents and brothers with the wind and rain blowing, as soon as it stops, they will be fine."

Then they quit spraying the water and turned off the fan to show her .... "See, don't you feel better now? Your family will be just fine." I thought that was a clever visual effect for teenagers to contrive at least.

"Did it help?" I asked.

"NO!" Lori replied.

Then she continued. She said at first, it had really just made her madder and more upset because she was still terrified by watching the TV and seeing all the devastation in the area where we were. She felt so helpless not being able to do anything and being so far away from us. Then she said that, after a few deep breaths though, she was able to appreciate what they were trying to do for her, and it did give her a little giggle for a split second and helped her feel a little better. She did have to confess that after she had gotten in touch with us and knew we were okay, she was actually glad to still have been in California then and not with us when it was all going on. She would have hated not having electricity or water for so long. It would have driven her crazy not being able to shower and wash her hair whenever she wanted to.

Younger girls always seem to take more than one shower a day, and I did know she would have been miserable not being able to do that. I certainly understood. It was not fun feeling so hot and sweaty after working out in the yard most of the day. I was temptedto jump in the lake more than once! We did have a little clean water in the tank in the RV though, and we were able to at least wash our faces and hands and quickly rinse off once in a while, so that was good.

When we finally were able to get in touch with Gary's sister, she told us about their experience. It was horrible for them during the time the hurricane passed through the area where they had gone to stay. First, they shared the good news their house had miraculously made it through without any major damage. They returned home and could live in it while repairs were happening. Great news from them we were happy to hear, especially after they told us what happened while they were in the hotel in Florence when the hurricane had reached the area where they were.

The hotel they'd checked in, hoping to be safe, became a target for the hurricane! The force of the winds had stripped the roof off and parts of the building had been torn away. The building was open all around and with all the hard rain blowing and coming in, it was filling up and began to rise, flooding the lower floors. Everything had gone black, and they were wet and scared. They had to crawl and feel their way down steps and through the remainder of the building to get outside and wait for help to come. I shuddered trying to imagine their fear while crawling through the water in the dark and all the while not knowing if the rest of the building was going to collapse and perhaps trap them inside. Just hearing the different sounds must have only added more fear and uncertainty to what the outcome of the situation might be.

They did make it out of the building and were taken to a shelter where they could get blankets and something to drink and be safe. By the grace of God, no one was seriously injured and there were no deaths in the hotel. Their belief and faith had gotten them through and kept them moving on while being so scared. When they were able to return home safely, they were relieved to find it still standing with just minor damage. They were blessed and thankful to have a home and not a disaster. We all had so very much to be thankful for.

Later, when we were able to travel to see them and offer our help, we just couldn't take in all the damage that had been done all along the more than three hundred miles between us and the coast. Everywhere you looked trees were stripped from where they used to be. Acres after acres were bare where beautiful fields of corn and other crops had been growing. The splintered remains of trees were sticking up like jagged matchsticks here and there. It felt eerie as if we were on another planet.

When we arrived at the ocean, we saw that instead of

the nice sandy beaches, the shore was covered with black lava-looking rocks. What everyone was used to running on, lying on and soaking up the sun, and building sandcastles and little pools when the waves washed ashore didn't exist. Many people didn't realize this hard black rock was under all the sand. It didn't seem possible all the white sand had been blown or washed away during the hurricane hours. Tons of sand would have to be hauled in or dredged out of the ocean to get the dunes rebuilt and enough sand back on the beach to cover the rock. This had been quite an experience of devastation for so many in different ways.

Scary and devastating times are never pleasant to experience, but even through those times, you see good happening all around you. Most of the time everyone arrives at better times afterwards. We are not promised there will never be hard times in life, but we are promised that with our belief in Jesus, we are not alone; we will get past each difficulty we face as God will allow.

"Be merciful to me, O God, be merciful to me,
for in you my soul takes refuge; in the shadow
of your wings I take refuge, till the storms of
destruction pass by."
--Psalm 57:1-2 (ESV)

CHAPTER 32: Another Kind of Storm

"You will keep whoever's mind is steadfast in
perfect peace; Because he trusts in you."
--Isaiah 26:3 (ESV)

Our first year in North Carolina passed by quickly. The boys were now in their first year of high school. They attended North Mecklenburg High School located in Huntersville, North Carolina. Happily, they had tried out for the school soccer team and made the cut. This meant getting to know the guys on the team better. Next, they were required to get a sports physical, to show they were healthy and fit to play. After being referred to the doctor who handled the school physicals, we had made an appointment for each of our boys. After the examinations, we waited for the results.

When they called, we were asked to bring Jake back to discuss a concern they had discovered from one of the tests. After an appointment was scheduled, we were a little anxious, but we didn't think it would be anything serious. Jake was a strong, healthy boy.

During the appointment, the doctor explained they had found blood and protein in his urine during a microscopic test, and he was concerned. So, he referred us to a nephrologist in Charlotte for a second opinion. My hopes were that this doctor would give Jake some medicine to take care of the problem and all would be well.

But instead of a prescription, the nephrologist set up more testing. This included additional lab work, an ultrasound, and CT scan of his kidneys. After studying the results of the tests, we were told he'd been scheduled for a biopsy of his kidneys. It would be outpatient surgery in Charlotte at the Carolinas Medical Center. Now we were getting worried! Why would they do a biopsy? He had never been sick or had any pain that would indicate he had a problem with his kidneys.

After all, Jake was just starting high school. He should only be thinking about enjoying life, having fun with his friends, playing soccer, boating, and fishing. But here he was thinking about having a biopsy of his kidney and becoming concerned thinking there must be something wrong if this was necessary. He was such a great young man, always so caring and wanting what was best for others. He was happy and wanted everyone else to be happy, too. It didn't seem fair that something might be medically wrong inside his seemingly very healthy body.

Even though he had not said anything, I knew he was worrying about having the biopsy. It would not be a pleasant experience for him. He had never been in a hospital before, let alone thought about having a very large and long needle enter through his back and reach to his kidney to remove small pieces to be examined. The end result should be a diagnosis for the cause of the blood and protein discovered in his soccer physical. On the day of the procedure, we drove to the hospital in Charlotte. I became emotional when they were taking him back to prepare him for surgery. Suddenly, it became too overwhelming. More than anything, I wanted to change this for him and shelter him from what might be ahead in his young life.

I managed to compose myself with Gary's help, although I knew he was just as worried about Jake as I was. We were told we could spend a few minutes with him before he was taken to the operating room. He would be awake with only a local anesthetic to numb the area. I wished they could have given him something, so he would not hear everything going on or that we could be with him to talk with him and keep his mind off everything that would be happening. But, of course, we knew that wasn't possible. We could only return to the waiting room and pray while we waited. We'd been told the procedure would take a little over an hour. As soon as it was completed, we'd be told how everything went and when we could visit him in the recovery room.

During moments like these, you want time to speed up so you can see that your loved one is doing well and hoping to hear they will be fine; it's nothing serious and all will be back to normal. But times of waiting for this type of news dragged by. Five minutes seemed like an hour or two. The clock seemed to move in slow motion.

The medical staff had kept us informed about the procedure, and then reported that all had gone well. Soon, we could see him in the recovery room. Finally, when we walked into the room, we were relieved to see Jake sitting up with his customary big bright smile.

He immediately began talking excitedly telling us, "Guess what? Rob's Mom was the nurse and stayed with me through the whole procedure!"

Rob was one of Jake's first good friends he'd made after

moving to North Carolina. He'd spent time at their house and liked Rob's mother. Even though he'd known she was a nurse, he never imagined she would assist during his biopsy.

What a special blessing! Even though Gary nor I could be with him, he'd been comforted by someone he knew well and who cared about him. This was special for our son and for us. When Jake was released, we returned home with instructions for him to rest. We'd be called for a consultation after they'd reviewed the biopsy. The uncertainty of it continued for him and for us.

The medical term when blood is detected in the urine is *hematuria*. There are two types of hematuria. The first is *gross hematuria*, when a person can see the blood in his / her urine; the second is *microscopic hematuria*, when looking at the sample through a microscope shows the blood. This was how Jake's was detected.

For our son, it would be life-changing, as we later learned when we returned to discuss the findings. The doctor explained Jake had a disease called *IgA Nephropathy* (Berger's Disease). There was no cure for this condition. He explained it is an autoimmune disease that attacks the kidneys and affects how blood is filtered in the blood vessels of the kidneys. The kidneys can begin to stop functioning and lead to kidney failure for some people. Others won't experience any complications at all, and the disease may even go into remissions on its own. However, some people develop more complications as the condition progresses.

Our seemingly healthy son was one of those people who would have the complications to include high blood pressure, high cholesterol, chronic kidney disease, acute kidney failure, possible heart problems, and end-stage renal disease, meaning that he would need a kidney transplant one day. We were devastated as we heard this. How could it be true? Jake was never sick; he was always healthy, big, and strong. He'd gotten worn out sometimes, but that was all. We never had any indication anything else was wrong.

Thank God for the doctor who gave him a thorough sports physical. We didn't know how long the disease may have been slowly destroying his kidneys and what might have happened if the physical had not been a requirement for high school soccer, and this had not been discovered. We learned the disease usually doesn't cause any symptoms and can go years or even decades without being detected. The blood found during a microscopic exam raised a red flag this disease could be a possibility, which is why further testing was required. We wanted to know how this happens; you just don't expect to hear a young person may have a disease like this. It seemed like something maybe your parents or grandparents may be diagnosed with but not your teenage son.

We needed more explanation to understand why this had happened to Jake. As far as we knew, there was no family history of anything like this in my family or in Gary's family. We felt so troubled and helpless and as if we weren't good parents by not knowing there was something going on with his health. The answers we began to learn were not a comfort. The fact was, researchers didn't know exactly what causes IgA Nephropathy. There seems to be both genetic and environmental components that cause it. A person can be born with a predisposition for the disease. Some type of *trigger* (an exposure to something or an infection) can occur and make the disease progress. If there isn't a trigger, there may never be a problem.

When I heard some trigger could initiate the disease, my mind immediately traveled to the day of the church picnic years ago in California. It had been a beautiful warm, sunny day when Jake and the children were running in and out of the lake, playing, and having a fun time together. That's when Jake was bitten by something indistinguishable, which caused his foot to immediately swell and become inflamed with infection. The urgent care doctor had examined him, gave him medication for the infection, and thought all would be well in a few days. He'd experienced no other symptoms, at least no warning signs that affected his health. There was no way of knowing his immune system had been weakened, allowing his kidneys to be attacked through the years and silently destroying them, resulting in kidney failure in his teen years. Until this disease was finally diagnosed, we never realized why he was tiring quickly and not being able to keep up with others when playing soccer

Our hearts broke for him, realizing what was ahead for his future. He was only fifteen. How long would it be before his kidneys ceased their job, and he'd need a transplant. Would he finish his high school years without being out of school for an operation? Would he and his brother be able to share all the fun events together? Would they be able to play on the soccer team together or go to proms and parties or enjoy summertime fun with friends? Would they be able to graduate from high school together? Twins have a close, unique relationship. These were events they'd always looked forward to enjoying together.

Jake, as always, faced it head on. He said, "We will just do what needs to be done when the time comes; there is no other choice."

It's a big wakeup call when your children have to remind you to have faith when you forget that you are not in control of certain things in life. Of course, he would rather it not be happening at all, but he always chose to stay positive about what was going on and to make the best of each day. His heart and his attitude were where all of ours needed to be and remain. We needed to be the stronger ones to support him during this time of uncertainty. He was continuing to live each day in the moment, and we needed to follow his example and not get him or us down talking about what was going to happen one unknown day.

There was no way to know when that day would be; only his body and the continued check-ups would determine the time. We were waiting for something we knew needed to happen, but we didn't know when. That was a hard pill to swallow at times. But remembering that God was in control, along with prayerful support from friends and family, we found comfort.

Even though we don't understand why things like this have to happened to our loved ones, knowing our Heavenly Father is always with us and keeps us as if in the palm of His hand, when we believe, trust, and obey His Word, he will see us through it all. We need to always put Him first and trust that he always has our best interest at heart.

"The Lord is near to all who call on Him,
to all who call on Him in truth."
--Psalm 145:18 (ESV)

CHAPTER 33: 1994 Celebrations

"Rejoice with those who rejoice,
weep with those who weep."
--Romans 12:15 (ESV)

Jake continued being on the school soccer team and played whenever he could, giving it his all. He and Jason had great times together with the team and all the friends they continued to make while in high school. He was able to go to all the school events and both the junior and senior proms. The continued checkups showed time was getting more critical, but he was able to graduate with his brother and classmates in 1994. Gary and I were very proud parents that day when our sons graduated together. It was a great time of celebration.

As a special graduation surprise, Gary and I had gotten tickets to take them to the World Cup Soccer Tournament, which was being played in Florida that year. Our tickets were to watch The Republic of Ireland and Mexico. We were really excited for Ireland. They had an outstanding victory against Italy in their previous match, allowing them to advance to this next round playing against Mexico.

Being Scots-Irish, of course we were cheering for Ireland. We had our big Irish flag hanging outside our hotel door showing our support. The Irish flag is made of three equal vertical sections with the green at the hoist, the white in the middle, and then the orange section. A group of French women sympathetic to the Irish cause had presented it to Ireland as a gift in 1848, designing it to symbolize the hoped-for union between Roman Catholics and Protestants, that divided northern and southern Ireland. The green represented the Catholic; orange represented the protestants; the white in the center signified a lasting truce between these two relationships.

The flag was not actually raised until the Easter Rising of 1916 in Dublin and has been used by nationalist on both sides of the border as the national flag of the whole island of Ireland today. It is a very colorful flag. Along with all the other hanging flags, this flag made for a festive sight all around the city.

The day of the game was greeted with very hot, scorching heat. Unlike most of the weather in Ireland but more like Mexico. When the game ended as a win for Mexico with a score of two goals to Ireland's one, we decided it was the heat that caused them to lose! We reasoned the team from Mexico was used to that type of heat and could hold up through the game without getting as worn out and tired. But all in all, it was a well-played game by both teams, and we enjoyed just being there. But, of course, we would have loved it more if Ireland would have won.

Lori had not been able to go with us because she was busy working. She had gotten a fun and enjoyable job being a merchandiser. She was also busy finishing up plans for an important day that was coming soon: Her wedding day! She had gotten engaged the previous year. The wedding was planned for August after the boys' graduation and after we returned from the trip to Florida. She didn't want her plans to interfere with the boy's excitement of graduating and going to the World Cup. We'd also planned to take them to Disney World and other vacation sites while we were in Florida, and Lori wanted to ensure that her brothers were rested and able to be in her wedding. We were happy for her and prayed she'd have a good life. I was happy she'd still be in the area and not be moving away to another state somewhere. I loved having my children close enough so we could all see each other whenever we wanted to without our having to drive a long time or fly somewhere to be together.

The timing worked out great. Jake and Jason could both be in her wedding. They loved their sister and were happy they could be there for her special day. I don't think Lori would have gotten married if her brothers could not have been part of her wedding. I could write another book about how beautiful she, as well as everything about that day was. I won't get carried away, but I will share that she thanked her dad and me for everything that made it so wonderful. "I truly felt like Cinderella," she had told us with tears.

That was actually very appropriate for Lori to say because when she was asked where she wanted to spend her honeymoon, she said, "Disney World!" To Lori, going there and then to Epcot was like a mini around-the-world trip for her. She has always been a true Disney fan. It's her favorite place to go. Everyone is happy and in a great mood when they are at Disney. Who could blame her for loving it?

Not long after the wedding, Jason would be going off to college. We were busy shopping for all the things he would need. After visiting colleges, he'd decided to attend UNC-Greensboro. This made me happy because he wouldn't

be far from where we lived. I like knowing we would probably see him often, at least when he needed his dirty clothes
laundered, which was just fine with me. I would gladly do his
laundry, so I could see him.

After they moved out of our home, I loved seeing them
whenever they had time to come and visit. I used to always
tell them and still do, "If I ever win the lottery, which would be
hard to do since I never buy a lottery ticket, I will buy acres of
land in a beautiful setting and build a gathering house right in
the middle of the property. Then I would have four long drive-
ways branching out from the gathering house that would lead
to four nice, cozy houses. One house for Gary and me, one for
Lori and her family, one for Jake and his family, and one for
Jason and his family."

I think they know I wouldn't be a nuisance, at least I
hope they feel that way. Then when it was someone's birthday
or a holiday or any special occasion, all the family could be together by just driving from our houses to the gathering house
for a celebration. How perfect! Right? And it wouldn't be a
problem finding a parking place for any of us like it is at times
when you try to meet at restaurants for get togethers.

My favorite role in life is being a Mommy and a Grammy. I could be a big Mother Hen and have them all under
my wings forever, if it were possible. It is fun to dream about
having us all just a driveway away. Who knows? Maybe, it will
be like that in Heaven when we are all there one day. That's
exciting to think about.

I read a poem a long time ago by Martin David "Bux"
Buxbaum. He was a successful businessman who retired as
a communication and public relations director with the

Marriott Corporation. Buxbaum was also an honored poet. Many people live life trying to discover their purpose. Truly, I have always believed my purpose was to be the mother of the children with whom I was blessed. In his short poem, Buxbaum lists some of the ways many people may define or measure success. There are many. Some think having a large home is success. Others may think obtaining that dream car is success. And still others may believe if their closets are full of designer clothes, they have achieved success. But in the final four lines of his poem, he defines how I hope I can be seen as successful in my purpose.

> *"...but the measure of your real success*
> *is one you cannot spend.*
> *it's the way your son [children] describes you*
> *when he's talking to a friend."*

I had told Gary while we were making plans and discussing the different things happening within our family that I wanted to be the one to donate a kidney to Jacob when it was time. I had always been healthy and was still young enough to be able to do this. I was not worried in the least that anything would go wrong. Also, it made more sense for him to be able to continue working and care for us. I was just working a part-time job to have something to do, and it would not be a hardship if my pay didn't continue for a while. His job was necessary because of insurance coverage too.

Another reason I wanted to do this first was because we had been told that the disease Jake had would also begin attacking the new kidney, which meant that one day, he would need a second transplant. When that would be necessary could not be known, and we prayed that my kidney would last a long time for him. I was a good match, but not a perfect match. Sadly, there was no way of knowing the length of time before it too would start to fail. I hoped when it was time that maybe Gary would be able to donate the next one. He had always been in good health and maybe would not be working as much then. It just made sense for me to do it first.

It wasn't long after Lori's wedding and Jason was settled in Greensboro that Jacob's next checkup indicated it was time for him to get a transplant. He was nineteen years old. Four years had passed since he was told he'd would need a transplant one day. That time was now. It was answered prayers that he was able to get through all the events of the previous four years without getting too sick or unable to be part of all that had taken place. God's timing is always perfect! I had informed the transplant team before that I wanted to be the donor, so they called and started setting up the appointments to get the required tests done to determine if I could be the donor. It takes a while to complete everything, so things were scheduled right away.

We were anxious for the results in case I couldn't be the donor for some reason so there would be time for others to be tested, who had offered to be a donor if we needed someone else. I had every confidence that I would be a match, but it was such a blessing to know we had others who were more than willing to be tested if needed. My motherly instinct and my faith were strong about it all. There was no question in my mind from the time I told Gary I wanted to be the one to donate the first kidney to Jacob that I would not be able to do this, I was very much at peace about it all.

We also wanted things to go quickly so Jake would not have to be on dialysis before the surgery if it could be avoided. We did not like the thought of him having to go sit for hours several times a week having waste, chemicals, and fluid pumped from his body while being so young and not be able to be out and about while he could with his friends. No one wants their teenager to have to go through that if it could be avoided or any loved one for that matter.

The necessary procedures that needed to be done had begun with a comprehensive physical and psychological evaluation. I was a little shocked about having a psychological evaluation, but when they explained why, I could see the important reasons it was necessary. Some people may get pressured into this by family when they really don't want to be a donor for some reason. That was something they wanted to ensure was not happening. If it were something they did discover, or if the potential donor had been bribed, they needed to address it. They would then help anyone in a situation where he/she felt trapped to decline in a way that would not cause hard feelings between family or others that might be involved in the situation in some way.

After the physical and psychological evaluation were completed and found to be acceptable, other testing would begin. One key element was the tissue typing. This is necessary to be done to ensure my blood group was compatible with Jake's blood type, so there would not be an acute rejection or irreversible graft loss on the operating table, which could result in an immediate rejection.

There would then be urine samples taken to screen for

any abnormalities or infection and a 24-hour sample collection to check the amount of protein and a creatinine clearance to determine adequate kidney function.

Also required was an intravenous pyelography test that involves an injection of dye into the vein which circulates through the body, into the kidneys, and then into the urinary tract with x- rays being taken to identify the structure of the kidneys, arteries, ureter, and other anatomy making sure all were healthy. During this procedure, I did get a little nervous. I could feel the dye moving all through my body and it felt very, very hot. I remember thinking if this doesn't end soon, I might just explode. I had to take some deep breaths and calm myself. It's crazy how our mind can start playing tricks on us if we let it. I started singing songs in my mind to keep it busy. Then all was well. I can't remember all the songs I was singing to keep my mind off the feeling I was having, but the music did the trick to keep me calmer and to quit thinking I was going to explode from the heat filling my insides!

The last procedure was a Helical CT scan, which is used to evaluate the internal structure of the kidneys and look for presence of cysts or tumors or any other problems. All these tests could not be done in one day, but they did work to get me in quickly, and all tests were performed in a timely manner so results could be studied as soon as possible. The disease inside Jake was working fast now. The results were studied, and I was thrilled to hear I would be a good match and could be the donor to give my son more years of life. The timing of it all had been amazing. It was a perfect chain of events the way it all worked out. When the results came, it was necessary for the surgery to take place.

"There is an appointed time for everything,
A time for every event under heaven."
--Ecclesiastes 3:1 (NAS)

Jake and Jason together at their
high school graduation.

CHAPTER 34: Kidney Transplant

"Even though I walk through the darkest valley,
I will fear no evil, for you are with me...."
--Psalm 23:4 (NIV)

The surgery date was set for September 13, 1994. On the previous day, we were at the hospital for what is called a bleeding time test. This test is needed to ensure the platelets are functioning correctly and to determine how quickly the blood clots from when the patient is cut to the time the bleeding completely stops. This assessment requires that the patient's arm is positioned at the level of his heart. A blood pressure cuff is placed on the upper arm and inflated to 40 mmHG, which is considered a normal and healthy pulse pressure, allowing the blood to flow normally. An incision is then made on the forearm and the cuff is removed.

A stopwatch is started immediately and every 30 seconds the blood is wiped off the cut and timed then repeated until the bleeding completely stops. This is to know what to expect with bleeding when the patient is cut open for the transplant and to be prepared if the patient's blood does not clot quickly because they are what is called a long bleeder.

This was being explained to us while we were sitting together in the room where they would do the test. Jake and I were sitting on chairs next to each other. Gary was standing next to me. We were talking to each other as the nurse was getting things ready. Jake was looking toward us, and it was good we'd be able to talk to each other to take his mind off what was happening. The nurse told him she would let him know before they would start to make the cut, so he would know to remain still and not jerk his arm.

Jake was still facing us and listening to me as I was commenting on something he had said when I noticed he was starting to look pale. His eyes began looking glassy. I had just asked, "Are you okay?" Without any warning or chance for us to catch him, he collapsed and fell hard onto the floor. I knew he had fainted. I jumped up and tried to get him to talk to me and regain consciousness. He had fainted once before a long time ago, but he came to right away. This time he was not. He remained unconscious, and I had seen that he had lost control of his bladder when he lost consciousness and collapsed.

I knew this had not happened before, and I was scared for him. Actually, I was panicking. Gary tried to remain calm in order to help me not be so upset, but I know he was as scared as I was. Suddenly, three doctors rushed into the room and began attending to Jake.

One of the nurses quickly took Gary and me out of the room and into another room, explaining someone would be back with us as soon as possible. It seemed like forever until they came back to talk to us. It was so difficult to be in that room and wait and not know what was happening to Jake. Finally, one of the doctors came to talk to us. He immediately let us know Jake was conscious and they were admitting him into the hospital for observation. We would be able to see him soon. The doctor wanted to give us a chance to calm down, explain what had occurred, and to reassure us Jake was fine. They also wanted to ensure there were no blood-clots, and his heart rate was okay to go ahead without any danger. This overnight observation was just a precaution to ensure nothing would delay the transplant in the morning.

He said what Jake had experienced was a vagal response to what was going on, namely being cut to check the clotting time of the blood. The vagal response involves the central nervous system, the peripheral nervous system, and the cardiovascular system being compromised. He explained further that when the reflex is triggered, it causes an abrupt drop in blood pressure and a sudden reduction in the heart rate. The blood vessels in his legs widened, which caused blood to pool in his legs, causing a reduction of the amount of blood flowing to his brain. This is what caused him to pass out, and his heart had stopped beating for a short time. The medical term is called vasovagal syncope. I praise God that they got his heart going quickly before any further complications occurred.

For those of you who don't know medical terms, like we didn't at the time, it is, in part, something we probably have all done at one time or another: fainted. However, usually when we faint, we regain consciousness in about a minute and most of the time we do not lose bladder or bowel control. Our heart pauses for only a short time -- not for the period of time that Jake's had stopped beating.

When we saw him in his room, he was resting and his color was back. They were taking good care of him. It was getting later by then, and they told us they would keep him comfortable and continue to monitor him all night. They advised us to go home and get some rest. If the surgery was going to continue as scheduled for the morning, I needed to be at the hospital very early to be prepped so the Doctor could harvest my kidney to be ready to transplant into Jake.

Well, I wasn't going for that. I wouldn't have to worry about getting there early because I was going to stay right there all night in his room. I planned to sit on a chair right next to his bed and watch to ensure he was breathing all night long. They did not argue with me. I sent Gary home to make sure everything was good there. Hopefully, he would get some sleep before he, Lori, and Jason would arrive in the morning.

God was with us all night, and the scheduled transplant surgery would take place. Gary, Lori, and Jason, along with other family members and many of our friends and Jake's, were there to be our prayer support and to be with Gary and the kids while Jake and I were in the operating rooms during the procedures.

We had no doubt about the team of doctors we were blessed to have performing the operations. The transplant team at Charlotte Medical Center (CMC) was one of the best available. The team of surgeons included the current head of the transplant center there, a top transplant surgeon who had come to CMC from the Mayo Clinic. In addition, there was an outstanding young resident who had done his training at the Mayo Clinic. We had spent lots of time talking and meeting with them, and they made us feel like we were all family.

When Jake and I had been moved into the holding area where the operating rooms were, we had a second before being wheeled to opposite but adjoining rooms where we would each be operated on. We had time to connect through a loving look for one another. Our eyes did the talking for us. It was a very special moment between us. I had no fear at all, and I could feel he felt the same because of the peaceful look he had on his face. There was no trace of fear or worry at all. My heart was full. We knew we were in very capable hands that were being guided from above and that we had a strong team of prayer warriors not only at the hospital, but all over who were praying for us. How blessed we were. It was wonderful to have the calming assurance that all would be well and not to be afraid, to know we were being held in the palm of God's hand. He would be directing the surgeons' hands through every second of the procedures taking place.

After the anesthesia had been given to us and we were told to start counting, it took no time before we were both in that blissful deep sleep you get when being put under. For me it's the kind of sleep that when you start hearing your name, as they are trying to awaken you, you just wish they would leave you alone, so you could enjoy it all a little while longer. One of the surgeons would first operate on me, removing my left kidney. They would start by laying me on my right side with my head and feet being positioned slightly lower than the rest of my body in order to make the removal of the kidney easier for them. The left kidney is preferred to be removed for the transplant because of the implantation advantages of having longer vessels and being more accessible to remove.

The surgeon would then make approximately a twelve-inch incision, starting on the front of my belly and up to the ribs. After the necessary muscle, fat, and tissue are cut out of the way, he would then remove my twelfth rib to provide more room for the process of removing the kidney. (Ironically, I think about how God removed a rib from Adam to create

Eve.) The tube that carries the urine from the kidney to the bladder and blood vessels are then cut away from the kidney. At that time, the kidney would be removed and taken to the adjoining operating room where the transplant surgeon was prepared for Jake to receive the kidney.

The procedure to remove one of my kidneys would take a total of three hours. I just wished that I would have thought to tell them to please feel free to go right ahead and cut out all the fat they found while they were in there. That would have been fabulous. I would not have minded that at all!

Jake had been prepared by his surgeon by making incisions in the lower part of his abdomen on his right side where the new kidney would be placed. They did not remove the old kidneys, as was the practice, unless there had been any infection, kidney stones, or anything that would have caused a problem during the operation. His kidneys had pretty much shriveled up like raisins and would be no problem if left in place.

It is actually good when they can be left to avoid having to make more cuts to remove additional muscle out of the way, which would result in more bleeding for the patient, and that was something they wanted to avoid if possible, so we were thankful there was no infection or stones to make it necessary to remove his old organs.

When the new kidney was placed in him, the blood vessels that had been removed with it would then be attached to the blood vessels in his abdomen This new kidney would be placed just above his leg, and the ureter tube of the kidney would then be attached to his bladder. It sounds so simple describing it on paper, but his surgery would also take about three hours to complete.

After both surgeries were completed, we had been sewn up, and our vitals were good, the doctors went out to let everyone know the surgeries were very successful. They were very excited about how well everything had gone. They assured everyone we were doing good and would be in the recovery room for a while. When we were settled into our rooms, they would be paged, so they could visit with us.

The staff suggested this would be a good time for them all to go get something to eat as it had been a long day, and they knew that most people waiting for news of their loved ones don't eat. They just drink lots of coffee.

I now know how hard it was for them to sit there and wait for all those hours. I would be on the other side of this same situation years later when instead of Jake and me, it would be Jacob and Jason being operated on at the same time.

After a time in the recovery room, we were being taken to our rooms, I was awake enough to realize they were taking me to one room at the far end of where they had taken Jake, not right next door like I had expected. They were separating us! We would not be close to each other; that just didn't seem right to me. I suppose they noticed my expression of not liking it, so they explained to me this was for our own good to help speed up our recovery. If we were close, we would not walk as much to see each other, and that was part of what helped us recover. Getting up and about and walking is always a good step toward recovery.

That was pretty smart of them. It would prove to make me get up and move sooner than I probably would have otherwise. I was anxious to see with my own eyes just how well Jake was doing. I figured out pretty quickly how to take my pillow and hold it against my side to make it more comfortable for me to be able to get up and hobble down the hall to see my son.

A day or so later, when I had walked to Jacob's room and gone in, he was just coming out of the bathroom and was doing so well getting around. He looked like a new person, not tired and worn out. He looked so healthy again. It was such a joy to see. We were both feeling great and joking about who had the biggest scars. We were just happy being together. I asked him, "Isn't it great how they were able to do this?"

I felt certain things were going to be so much better for him now. I shared with him that I felt this kidney would serve him well for longer than they do for some transplant patients. He smiled at me and said, "Oh, I know it will Mom. While I was in the bathroom just now, I gave a little prayer of thanks, and I heard the angels singing that all was well. I have many great years of good health ahead for me."

How wonderful to hear my son believed and recognized this assurance from God who is so good to us.

"But let all who take refuge in you be glad,
let them ever sing for joy. Spread your protection over
them, that those who love your name may rejoice in you."
--Psalm 5:11 (NIV)

A little while later, the young resident, who I will call *Dr. H.* when referring to him from now on, came in to check on Jake and shared that it was his privilege to be on the team, and said this was his first assist since joining the staff at CMC, and he was so happy for us that everything had gone so well. He and Jake had developed a great doctor-patient relationship right from the beginning while meeting during the many appointments leading up to the actual surgery. We would be so thankful for this special bond in years to come when we would again need his help in a more desperate way.

Everyone at the hospital was being so wonderful to us while we were in there. I had recuperated too fast, I guess, because after a few days, they came to tell me that I would be able to go home. I was feeling really good and knew I would be fine at home now. The thing was, I didn't want to leave and go home without Jake. It brought back the feeling I had when the boys were born and I had left again while one son had to stay.

I told them I understood they needed to discharge me to free-up the room for another patient, but I did not want to leave. I asked if they could just bring a cot into Jake's room for me, so I could stay with him. I told them that I would need nothing else, and I would not get in their way when they were caring for Jake. I just wanted to stay and be there until he was discharged if I could. They said they would see what they could do.

Later that day, Dr. H. came in to talk with me. I was sure he would say they could not allow it; you know because of insurance reasons and all, but instead he said, "Hi Mom!" (He was calling me Mom, too, and I was old enough to be his mom, so it was nice to hear.) "The nurse told us you asked if you could get a cot and stay with Jake. Instead of that, we have made better arrangements for you. We are going to move you into the room right next door to Jake's. You will be treated as a patient until both of you can leave together."

I was in tears hearing this and for all the care, compassion, and kindness we'd received from everyone who was involved through this transplant process. The love and understanding was a true blessing that has never been forgotten to this day. The time we were there in September of 1994 was for a reason we would have chosen not to have ever happen in our lives, but it was a time we knew our God was with us every step of the way.

The reason for our move to North Carolina was clear: This wonderful team of transplant surgeons and this well-equipped Charlotte hospital, along with the doctor who gave Jake a physical for sports, were the ones God had planned to make this disease known and the transplant successful for Jake, and He had it all planned out as to how we would get here.

> *"Consider it pure joy, my brothers, and sisters, whenever you face trials of many kinds, because you know that the testing of your faith produces perseverance. Let perseverance finish its work so that you may be mature and complete, not lacking anything. If any of you lacks wisdom, you should ask God, who gives generously to all without finding fault, and it will be given to you. But when you ask, you must* **believe and not doubt***, because the one that doubts is like a wave of the sea, blown and tossed by the wind. That person should not expect to receive anything from the Lord. Such a person is double-minded and unstable in all they do."*
>
> *--James 1:2-8 (NIV)*

CHAPTER 35: Love is Shown in Many Ways

"And over all these virtues put on Love,
which binds all together in perfect unity."
--Colossians 3:14 (NIV)

We were going home a week later. Jake would have lots of changes to handle in his way of life now. But he was alive, thank God, and we all would take one day at a time and get him to feeling better and back to living his life, enjoying all that was out there for him to experience as healthy once again. He, along with our help when it was needed, followed all the instructions he had been given and took all the precautions needed to protect that new kidney and make sure it would not be rejected. There were new medicines he would need to take, and a journal to be kept charting daily temperatures, blood pressures, weight, and what foods he ate. There would be necessary changes in the food he would be able to eat now to not impede the different medicines he would be taking. The incision sites needed to be cleaned and dressed, and he was to note the amount of pain and tenderness of the area where his new kidney had been placed. It was important to note if he was retaining fluid or if there was a significant decrease in urine output. Any number of things could indicate his body trying to reject the kidney. We were to call and get to the hospital as soon as possible if they occurred.

For the first couple of weeks after coming home from the hospital, a home nurse was assigned to come to our house for visits a couple times a week to check on Jake and ensure all was going well, so we didn't have to go to Charlotte to have his vitals checked and his incisions examined and redressed. She was always so pleasant when she came. She always was efficient and assured us he was doing great.

There were no emergencies or scares that needed us to rush him back to the hospital. His recovery was going as expected, and we were so grateful for everything. There are changes to be concerned about and mindful of like with any surgery and change in medication. The medications he needed to start taking to fight against rejection are Cyclosporine and Prednisone. They need to be adjusted all the time to ensure they were working properly and not trigger the white blood cells to attack the kidney. Like many drugs that help one thing, they can cause other symptoms that are not pleasant sometimes. This, I think, is one of the hardest parts of living with a transplant. It seems unfair medications that are necessary to keep one thing working can cause other complications within a person's body.

Jake's immune system had already been compromised by the years this disease had gone undetected. His body would now have to fight off other diseases along the way that these medications could contribute to causing. Knowing that one day he would need another transplant was heartbreaking for us. As parents, you feel so helpless not being able to keep these added illnesses from happening. The list of common side effects that might occur from taking the anti-rejection medications seemed endless, but with all things one faces in life, you either accept what is necessary and learn to be thankful for the moment you are in, or you let yourself get down and make yourself miserable. It is all about your attitude and choice. There are always others out there who have and will have harder or more problems to cope with than we ever will. So, learn to appreciate and accept what you have to deal with and that it is not as difficult as others might have to go through.

Jake chose that way to handle his situation. As a result, he continued to get stronger and healthier and had more energy than he'd had in a long time. The medicine was working as it should, and he was able to get back to living and enjoying his young life. He would face having some restrictions and would have many follow-up appointments with continued testing throughout the years to ensure the kidney was staying healthy and working as it should. It was a lot for a young guy to take in and know it would be a part of his life forever. But he continued doing what he had to do, accepting all the changes as just what had to be done. Some of the changes were sad for him to have to realize and be mindful of when before he had not given them a second thought, like spending most of the day outdoors. The risk of skin cancer is higher when taking the medicine necessary to prevent rejection, so he would not be able to be out in the sun much anymore.

Unfortunately, over the years, he has had many skin cancers that needed to be cut out even though he is always careful not to be out in the sun for too long at a time. He has also needed to be careful about the many activities he had taken for granted before: his love of hiking, camping, and just exploring the beauty of nature. He loved spending all the time he could out in the world. He had talked many times about becoming a forest ranger one day but realized that may not be an option for him any longer. He had been a volunteer at the Carolina Raptor Center and loved working with the animals and learning all he could about them.

Jacob and Jason loved going together to hiking trails and riding their mountain bikes for miles and miles, enjoying the outdoors. They had always enjoyed spending many hours out on the lake, boating, fishing, and swimming with family and friends. Now, he could only be out for short periods of time and had to carefully protect the placement site of his new kidney.

When he and his brother were younger, they loved rescuing stray animals and bringing them home also. We seemed to have one kind or another of different little creatures coming to visit or stay with us throughout the years. Once, when they were in elementary school, the classroom had a snake inside a tank that was part of lessons learning about different creatures. The teacher had small feeder mice the snake was fed that the kids watched -- not something I would enjoy but a lesson on the cycle of life I suppose. At any rate, Jake had spotted a cute little black and white mouse that he did not want to see be eaten, so he asked the teacher if he could please take it home and take care of it and have it as a pet. The teacher checked with us, and after Jake promised to take good care of it, we said he could.

He came home all excited and happy with the little creature that day and fixed up a nice home for it in a small, empty aquarium we had stuck away after the fish phase had not lasted long. He set the aquarium on top of his dresser in his bedroom and named the mouse, *Squeak the Mouse*. He took good care of it and had fun with that little mouse. Squeak was having a great life and doing so well until the cat Jake had rescued (he named it *Meow the Cat)* started taking interest in the tiny mouse.

You are catching on to Jake's way of naming his rescued pets. I loved it! There was no need for fancy names. What they were and the sound they made were perfect names for them. Poor Squeak started being visited often by Meow. Even though Jake had put a piece of screen over the top of the aquarium so he would be safe, the cat would just push it aside and join the little mouse inside for a visit. Meow did not want to hurt Squeak, not at all; he just wanted to say hello, make him feel welcome, and play with him a little while.

Later, I guess, Meow wanted to show Squeak the rest of the house too because one day after going up for a visit, he came walking down the stairs with the mouse in his mouth. Scared of what had happened to the poor little mouse, we started toward Meow. Meow just gently sat Squeak on the floor and started tapping at him, so he would start running. Meow would then start chasing after Squeak for a little time of playing where there was more space to run around, showing how this was more fun than just standing inside a glass box with no room to move.

We had a good laugh and were amazed the mouse was not hurt at all; however, over time, we did notice the poor mouse was starting to lose his hair. We thought we had better begin closing Jake's door, so the poor Squeak didn't have a complete nervous breakdown from Meow wanting to play all the time with the little thing. I think Meow thought he had the best cat toy ever.

That cat was a character. He was a fluffy Norwegian

Forest Cat. He was big and mostly black but had white markings on him that made it look like he was wearing a tuxedo. He had been left behind in the neighborhood where we last lived in California when the previous owners moved away. He had decided to make his new home in the bushes that lined the sidewalk leading to our front door. He made himself known by attacking our legs when we walked past the shrubs to the front door. We learned to walk around another way pretty quickly after being ambushed a few times and having those sharp claws dig into our legs. He managed to draw lots of blood from us, and some of our friends too before we all got smarter. We did not run him off; we were animal lovers in every way and Jake had bowls of food and water all set up for him, so he would not be hungry or thirsty. He would talk to the cat and try to get him to come to him, but the cat was still mostly hiding.

He did eat the food and drink the water Jake always made sure to sit out each day for him, but he was still not sure about getting near us. After a time, he would be seen out from under the bushes more, looking around here and there, but still not willing go get close to us. Our garage door was usually open most of the day; the kids were always in and out getting bikes or skateboards or whatever they needed when they were outside playing, so it was just easier to leave it open until they came in for the evening.

One day Jake saw Meow a little closer, and he decided to make him a house out of a cardboard box that he found so the cat could come in the garage and be more comfortable. He got busy and cut a door in the box. Next, he made windows on the sides and even got some fabric scraps I had and dressed the windows with little curtains. He wasn't quite finished after he had done that. He came in and got an old fluffy towel and arranged it just right inside the cat house and finished it off by painting *MEOW THE CAT* in red paint over the door. He wanted this cat to feel welcome and know he had a place to stay instead of living in those old bushes and sleeping on the dirt.

Jake wanted this cat to be shown love after being left behind by his former family. It wasn't long before Meow knew he had found a good home. He had started enjoying that box house and realized it was safe to be around these people who lived in this house. Then Meow decided it might be even more comfortable inside the bigger house he saw us going in and out.

Shortly after that, when I opened the door going out into the garage, Meow was standing right there and cautiously made his way past me and into the house, taking one slow step after another until before long, he was exploring all around the rooms inside. Apparently, he liked it fine because he was there to stay after that.

It didn't take him long at all to make himself at home, jump on our laps, and enjoy being petted and scratched. He quickly became part of the family, and knowing Jake was the one who made it all possible, Meow became Jake's shadow. No matter who he was around or what he might be doing, if Jake came in or left the room, Meow was right with him. He made Jake's bed his bed too, and as long as Jake was in his room, he was right there cuddled up as close as he could get to him. He and Jake became best buddies. They were just really tuned into each other, and it was so sweet and cute to watch.

We were never really able to figure out how old Meow

may have been, but he did have some grey in his black hair and was missing quite a few teeth, so we weren't sure if he would be around very long, but whatever time he did have, we enjoyed having him as our pet. He was so much fun and always entertained us. It was like he could talk with his actions! We brought him and two other cats the boys rescued, along with us in the motor home when we moved to North Carolina.

Counting the two dogs that got to fly to North Carolina, we had five rescued furry babies. There was, of course, Meow, then Snooky and Missy, the other two cats, and the dogs' names were Blu, who was the big, white Lab, and Molly, our Australian Shepherd. They were all awesome pets. Rescue pets seem to know they were chosen to be a special part of the family who brings them home, and they return that love over and over.

Jake and Jason had found the baby kittens we named Snooky and Missy when they had gone up on a hill close to our house where they went to ride their dirt bike. There was a little cave on the hill, and one day they noticed meow sounds coming from inside and went in to explore. They found these two kittens alive and others already dead. They carried the two kittens home and begged to keep them. I had my doubts we could keep them alive, but we had them looked at by the vet. He told us it was doubtful they would make it, but if were willing to commit to 24-hour care, they might have a chance. He explained that we would need to feed them every two to three hours, just like having a newborn baby, with tiny bottles filled with formula of mother cat's milk and be like the cat mother to them, encouraging them to suck on the little nipple, burping them, and then stimulating them to urinate and defecate by using a moist cottonball to rub the kittens' anal area. This meant, of course, I would be up throughout the night doing that. I couldn't say no; the boys were so anxious to make sure they would be okay. They were in school, and I could not wake them through the night to do this. I wanted them to be rested for school each day. We bought everything that was needed and went home with the tiny little things not knowing if they would make it through the first night.

Our Lab, Blu, would let the tiny kittens cuddle up by her where she protected them and treated them with gentle care. Our beautiful white Lab was a seventy-pound giant next to them. The Vet said they were tiny three-ounce Maine Coon grey kittens only days old. Blu was so sweet taking care of them when they were nestled close to her. We, or I really should say I (too bad it hadn't been when school was out when the boys found them, or I would have made them get up every three hours with me) continued this routine for quite a while until the kittens caught on, learned to eat on their own, and started finding the litter box to go potty in. It was amazing and actually gratifying that they had made it and continued to thrive. (The rescued kittens, Missy and Snookie are below.)

Later as they got stronger and continued to grow, it appeared Meow had decided it was time for him to teach them to be like cats not just cuddle with dogs. The wise guy was really using them to his advantage. I discovered instead of helping them know they were cats, he wanted them to learn that cats were in charge, in particular, him – not dogs or people! He started jumping on them just to get them to make enough noise, so we would come and see what was going on. Then he would immediately jump up and run to the back door. As he turned and stared at us, he had a look that I'm sure if he could talk would be telling us, "If you would have been paying attention to me and see that I wanted to go outside, I would not have had to jump on the kittens to make them cry to get you to come in here and let me out. So, pay attention humans!"

I could almost imagine what his voice would sound like -- smart and bossy for sure. It still makes me laugh to think about it.

Meow usually wanted to go outside because the dogs were out in the back yard, and he wanted to go out and play with them. He would run back and forth with them, chase and run after balls, and then flop down on his back when they did to scratch his back like they were doing. He had all the dogs' moves down perfect; he was a true cat-dog I guess you could say.

You are probably wondering why I keep going on so much about him. We had all kinds of pets over the years, which were all special to us. We loved them equally, but there was just something a little special about Meow. I guess because he started out as such a rascal, a mean guy that liked to hurt us by clawing our legs as we walked past him when he was hiding in the bushes along our sidewalk. But then he became a joy for us, full of mischief, fun, and love when he knew we cared for him and gave him a home where he was loved in return.

I think of him like some of the examples of people in the Bible who were considered bad and awful but then became good people after learning about Jesus. They turned their lives around, being filled with love for others and spreading the love of God everywhere they went.

In the book of Acts in the New Testament of the Bible, you will read about Saul of Tarsus, a man filled with hate who persecuted Christians, men, and women, alike, until the day he was met by Jesus. He learned about him, believed in him, and became a changed man. He then became known as Paul the Apostle and spent his life spreading the word of God to all the people where he traveled.

Like our Meow, that once had been treated mean and wanted to hurt others because of hate, he had learned to be kind, to be loved, and to love others. This shows an example to me of how when we are changed, when we accept Jesus and believe in Him and obey the word, love is ever present and there for us to share with others.

I mentioned before that we really didn't know how old Meow was. He was around for quite a while before he became our cat that one day when he decided to enter our house in California after he learned to trust us. He may have been old, but he was not too old to change. He became a real treasure to us and especially to Jake.

When Jake and I left for the hospital that first day before the transplant was to take place, we told all our pets good bye, and we would be back soon.

We always did that, and we still do when we leave our dog, Eddie, that we have now. He is our very spoiled, black and white miniature golden doodle. I wanted another puppy so much, and he was supposed to be my little lap dog, but he betrayed me and became a daddy's boy, always being with Gary and fretting when Gary goes somewhere, even though I am home with him. I should have gotten a little girl puppy instead! Just kidding; Eddie is a joy to us both.

Our pets have always been part of our family, and we always said goodbye when we would leave the house without them. On this day before Jake's transplant, as we were telling the pets goodbye, the dogs wagged their tails and the cats rubbed against our legs and purred. Meow was as close to Jake as he could get until we were all finally out the door.

This was the day when Jake had that scary episode during the test to check how long it would take his blood to clot, and he and I both stayed that night at the hospital. Gary had gone home for the night, so he could bring Lori and Jason back with him in the morning. He called me when he had gotten home to tell me that Lori and Jason said that as soon as we left, Meow had gone up to Jake's room and had gotten under his bed. They tried every way they could to get him to come out, but he had moved back as far as he could against the wall. No matter what they did, they were unable to reach him or coax him out. Gary had also tried when he got home, but he could not get him to come out either. They left fresh food and water under the bed for him and brought a litter box up and placed it close, so Meow could get to it when he needed to use it. He just was not going to come out from under there for anyone. In fact, he stayed there the whole time we were in the hospital, well over a week.

Meow ate a little, they said, and seemed okay when Gary or the kids checked on him, but he still continued staying under the bed. We decided he was just really missing Jake and was waiting right there for when he came back home. Jake had stayed overnight with friends before and Meow didn't do that, but maybe Meow sensed that Jake was sick this time and just wanted to be where Jake slept when he was home for some kind of comfort.

The day we did come home with Jake from the hospital, we had gone into the house and went to the kitchen to sit down and have a glass of something cold to drink and rest a minute. After not moving around much for a while, climbing the steps to get inside made our weak legs a little sore, so we were taking it easy at first. I felt sure that Meow had heard Jake's voice as soon as Jake was inside, and we were all sitting at the table when we noticed Meow slowly walking into the room.

He went straight to Jake and cautiously jumped up on Jake's lap and began checking him out. He gently sniffed him and rubbed up against Jake, purring all the while. Jake was so happy to see him and glad to see that Meow had finally come out from under his bed. After Meow was satisfied that it was indeed his Jake back home, he appeared to be doing well, and all was well with him, he jumped down to the floor, slowly took a few steps toward the corner of the room from where Jake was sitting and laid down to breathe his last breath.

If that doesn't display the love animals have in their hearts, I don't know what does. It was a love story. Jake had shown Meow love and started taking care of him, and in return that cat showed his love for Jake. He loved him so much that he held on in his old age, long enough to see Jake one more time and to know he was going to be all right before he allowed death to free him of the pain he must have been in. We then realized that was why he stayed under the bed.

Animals try to go off by themselves to die when it is their time, but Meow hung on long enough to see Jake again and know he was okay. What a beautiful message about loving; no words were spoken by Meow, of course, but just by his actions, his message of love for others was shown in a huge way. That is why *Meow the Cat* was so special and is always remembered with love by us all.

That was more than twenty-eight years ago, and I still get tears in my eyes each time I think about it -- our whole family does. We got so much joy from that cat, and we share that story with new friends we make during our journey through this life. Don't ever try to tell me that animals are not capable of feeling emotions and are not able to love. All of God's creatures have a heart and love is in that heart. They deserve to be loved and cared for because they have an unconditional love like we should have for each other.

Just like people, they only become mean and hateful if they are taught that. If what surrounds them is neglect, being treated badly, and not being cared for, that is all they will know and how they will act, just as people do when they are treated this way. That was Meow; he had been treated badly and became mean, but when he was shown love and knew someone cared for him, his heart filled with love, and he returned that love in such a heart-warming way to our family, especially to Jake.

"But ask the animals, and they will teach you,
or the birds in the sky, and they will tell you;
or speak to the earth, and it will teach you, or
let the fish in the sea inform you. Which of all
these does not know the hand of the Lord has
done this? In his hand is the life of every crea-
ture and breath of all mankind."
-- Job 12:7-10 (NIV)

All living and breathing things were created by God, and love is what He wants for all. God's motive is Love, His Word, His way! His Life is LOVE!

(Shown below is Meow the Cat with his Christmas bow in a box surrounded by tissue.)

Our beloved pets:
Meow, Molly and Blu.

CHAPTER 36: A Second Transplant Needed

"He comforts us in all our affliction, so that we may be able to comfort those who are in any affliction."
--2 Corinthians 1:4A (ESV)

Seventeen years had gone by since Jacob had his first transplant at the age of nineteen. As you can imagine, there were many events, which occurred over these years. Jake and Jason had both gotten married and had children. They made good homes for their families. Lori had divorced when her first son was only three months old. She and Garrett came to live with us for a while until she could get back on her feet, later moving into a condo not far from our house. Many events that seem to happen in life always include some good and some not. Divorce is sad, but sometimes it seems like it is the best thing considering the circumstances.

It looked like Jacob would soon be needing a second kidney transplant. We were thankful the first one had lasted for seventeen years. Some transplants last only a few years, so we were thankful for the time it had functioned in his body. Now, however, signs were beginning to show that the disease inside of him had been working to destroy the kidney once again.

He was beginning to feel bad and becoming sick easier. His primary doctor felt it was time for him to begin to see a nephrologist again. We did know this would happen again one day, but you're never really prepared for it when it actually does happen.

Charlotte and the surrounding areas had grown a lot during the previous seventeen years, and many new medical centers had been opened all over the area. In the town where we then lived in Mooresville, North Carolina, a new Nephrology Center had been built. Jake was referred there and would begin seeing the doctor for checkups leading to the time the new transplant was needed. It did make it convenient not having to go all the way into Charlotte for all the appointments that were needed because traffic was so congested with all the growth.

The actual transplant surgery would still take place in Charlotte at CMC where the first one had been, but until a time was scheduled, he would be able to go to the local Kidney Center in Mooresville.

Of course, Gary, Lori, and Jason were all more than willing to be tested to be the donor this time for Jake, but it had been determined that Jason would be the best match, being the same age and being so healthy. Gary was healthy, but older now, and a younger kidney was better. Lori had thyroid cancer and had to have the cells destroyed by radiation therapy, so she wasn't a good candidate, plus she had a baby to take care of now. So thankfully, Jason was able to be considered for the donor.

I truly believe God had foreseen all of this, thirty-six years earlier, and His plan was now being confirmed, proving that He knows all and is in control of providing what He knows we will need. Our Father has the most perfect plan at the exact right time when it will be needed most. In His Time!

The fact I delivered two baby boys that night in 1975 was indeed a big surprise to us all, but the fact that one baby had been conceived three weeks before the second one and the fact that the first baby conceived would one day need a second kidney transplant and the second baby was miraculously placed in the womb was nothing less than a miracle. The fact the second baby would grow alongside him and share a wonderful life growing up and be there to provide the second, healthy, perfect kidney to his brother to save him and give him more time to live here on earth was nothing less than another miracle from God—Nothing is impossible with our God.

Jason began the testing and was proved to be the match we were praying for. Being siblings, the same age and being a perfect match, the longevity for this kidney when placed in Jacob and God willing, could last Jacob the rest of his life.

I read several articles about brothers giving brothers kidneys and found there are brothers living today who had the same experience in 1977. One brother gave another brother a kidney that was a perfect match. Both men are healthy and doing great to this day, which is over forty-five years ago, and the kidney continues working and doing its job.

I continued researching after reading this and found that the longest surviving kidney transplant patient from a sibling is fifty-six years. Who knows, maybe my boys will be the new record holder one day. It could very well happen. When it does though, someone else will probably have to write about it. I am pretty sure I will not be able to sit here, type, and share that great news. But if I am still here and able to write about it, I can be a record holder too!

I knew Jake was so thankful for the perfect living donor being his brother, but I sensed he was feeling bad about the operation his brother would have to go through in order to do this for him. Thankfully, we would learn the surgery was less invasive for the donor now than it was before when I was the donor. The procedure was now done as a laparoscopic donor nephrectomy instead of requiring a major surgery that had resulted in more pain and a longer recovery for patients back in 1994. That was great news for us. I knew Jake was so happy that Jason would not have as much pain and would be able to get back out and about again sooner than we had all thought.

When you have a living donor available, the surgery should be scheduled and take place as soon as possible. We were hoping for another experience like the first time he received a transplant, where everything had proceeded from beginning to end on a perfectly timed schedule. There was no delay, no patient / doctor, or I guess I should say mother of patient / doctor doubt and uncertainty about the care given, and no other health problems along the way before the actual transplant day. Jake would not have the same experience at all this time.

As it turned out, Jake had many hard years before the transplant was finally scheduled. He was living with Gary and me, along with his son, Liam, now while he wasn't doing well. He and his wife had divorced, and Jake had begun to get sicker and was not able to work. We didn't want him and Liam to live alone.

Several unforeseen health problems occurred as his

kidney failure progressed. He had started seeing the nephrologist right away when a problem was detected at the beginning, but it seemed like his immune system was not able to fight off any type of sickness at all. Each time he went for a check-up, the nephrologist would send him to a different specialist to check for another potential problem.

Nothing seemed to help, and instead of results for the better from all the other doctors he saw, Jake never got healthier, it seemed. In fact, he had even been admitted into the hospital a couple of times because he had gotten so sick. They just kept putting him on one different type of medication after another, which seemed to only cause more problems mixed with his current medications. This delay along with additional problems was not giving his body a chance to get strong enough for surgery.

Gary and I were getting very concerned about what he was going through, and I have to admit, I was truly beginning to doubt the care the local nephrologist was providing Jake. It didn't seem right that he was being passed around from one doctor to another, ending up in the hospital and not getting any results that made his health improve enough to be able to have the transplant he needed! My doubts grew when Jake had to be put on dialysis because he had gotten worse. This was not right; his brother was there and had been ready to donate the kidney to him long ago. By this time, I was not just concerned and full of doubt, I was getting very upset and mad about what was going on. My mother's intuition was not letting me rest as I thought about it.

Jake could see my frustration, especially when a call I made to the nephrologist about some concerns I was noticing about Jake's health was not returned. It was the only time I had placed a call to this doctor to ask a question, and I was very upset about not getting a call back. Jake, being the person he was, calmly told me, "Mom, I am not his only patient; he is very busy. He will get back with us when he can."

I tried to settle down and not make my son feel worse by my complaining. The doctor never called back, it wasn't until Jake's next appointment that I went along and was able to ask about my concerns and not being happy about how it was all being handled. All the previous visits and Jake being on dialysis had been going on a year and a half since he was first told he needed a second kidney transplant. This should not have been happening; the transplant should have taken place right away when Jason was tested and was found to be the match needed. A delay this long was unacceptable, and he should never have needed to be on dialysis nor be sent around to one type of doctor after another.

Gary shared all of this with one of his friends later, and he told Gary he had met a retired transplant surgery at an event he had attended and would be glad to give him a call and see if he would be willing to meet with Gary to discuss his thoughts about what was going on. The surgeon was glad to meet with Gary and would be able to in a few days, after the Easter weekend. I was glad we would be able to get his input on the situation Jake had been experiencing.

Gary and I had gone to church on Easter Sunday. When we returned home, I went to change my clothes. Gary came back in a little while to do the same, and I noticed he had tears running down his cheeks. I asked what had happened, and he said that Jake had come out to talk with him. He shared their conversation.

Jake had said, "Dad, will you take care of Liam if I won't be able to do it?"

Gary answered, "Of course, I will Jake. You know Mom and I will always be here to help all of you in any way we can when any of you need anything."

Gary's response was given because he thought Jake was talking about his recovery time after the transplant. He wouldn't be able to get Liam what he might need. Then he told me what Jake had meant. Jake's answer was, "I know that Dad, but I don't think I'm going to make it."

Hearing this from our son, the young man who always tried to stay positive until now, who never blamed others for what might be going on and being patient with the doctor when we hadn't been, had just shared with his dad that he felt like he may be dying and would not get healthy enough to get the transplant he needed to go on.

This was like a stab in our hearts, knowing he was feeling this way. He was not saying he was afraid to die; he was making sure his son would be taken care of and not have any struggles in life without his dad being here with him. The feeling that came over me then is something I can still feel when I think of it now. Tears always fill my eyes, just thinking about Jake's loss of hope – how he had to have been feeling at that moment.

"This cannot be happening," I prayed. "Something has to be done and done soon."

This wasn't God's plan for my son. I just felt it with all my being. Gary's friend set up a meeting for Gary and the retired surgeon. The doctor said that as soon as Jason was approved for a match, the surgery should have been scheduled right away.

His words to Gary were, "It should have been a slam dunk!" He went on to tell Gary that just because Jake had been seeing a doctor here in North Carolina, it did not mean that we could not go to another hospital in a different state for the surgery. He was no longer licensed to practice since he retired, but he still knew many great transplant surgeons where he had moved from, and he would be more than happy to call and get it set up with them if we were willing to travel to another state.

After hearing that, I was not waiting any longer to try to make something happen here in Charlotte. I was concerned about Jake being able to travel to another state, but I was determined to figure out something, so Jake would not be going back to the nephrologist that he had been going to. I hoped I was wrong, but the only results I ever saw at that center were patients just being put on dialysis, and as long as that was happening, it seemed good enough. I could not accept that for my son, who had so much more life to live.

I told Jake I was going to see if I could get in touch with Dr. H., the young resident who was on the team during Jake's first transplant and whom we had grown to think so much of. I hoped we could talk with him about our concerns and get something done here in Charlotte. I called, explained to the scheduling nurse the situation, and she scheduled an appointment for us to be able to meet with Dr. H. that very week.

On the day of the appointment, as soon as we walked into his office, we felt the instant connection of friendship and trust we had established all those years before with this wonderful, caring doctor. Jake was all smiles when he saw him, and the doctor gave us both a big hug. He told us to sit down, and after we had, he looked at me and said, "What's wrong Mom? Why did you want to come and talk to me?"

I could hardly get out my reply. With tears streaming down my face, I said, "I think they are going to let my son die."

I could see by the shocked expression on his face that he had not expected me to say that, and he did not like what he was hearing at all as we shared our concerns. Jake and I both shared about how his brother was a perfect match and that was a year and a half ago. The surgery should have been scheduled then. We shared that Jake kept getting sent to one doctor after another for different things to have checked out without anything really being resolved; he had just been given more medication and was getting worse instead of better.

"Gary and I do not feel he is being taken care of properly," I said, "This has resulted in Jake having to be on dialysis."

Then Jake told him that he was losing hope he could make it long enough to actually get another transplant. Things were quiet. I didn't know what to say any further and didn't know what would happen next.

During the time Dr. H. had been at CMC, almost nineteen years at the time, he had been promoted within the transplant department and did not see patients until the transplant had been scheduled as part of the transplant team. We had been thankful for just the chance to talk with him at this point to get his input on everything and to ask if he had any suggestions as to what we should do to get Jake well, so the transplant could take place soon.

Instead of just listening and giving us his opinion after

hearing what we had shared with him, he looked at us and said, "You know I do not see patients in my office anymore, but as of this minute up until and through the surgery, until Jake is fully recovered and doing well, he will now be my only patient coming to my office. And he will see no other doctor but me through it all.

We had not expected this. We knew all the additional responsibility he now had, and we were amazed that he was going to do this for Jake. Well, I guess not really amazed, as I said before, we felt like a real friendship, a bond almost like being part of a family, had been established during the time of the first transplant. This had verified how special that connection still was when it came to Jake's care.

A door that had been opened years ago, led to this day that would begin the long-awaited process to ensure Jake would get the help he needed, so the transplant would finally take place. Not only were we thankful for this loving medical care that was now available, but also for the much-needed gift of hope that was restored to Jake by seeing that he was going to be given a chance to receive the healthy kidney from his brother after all. He would be given more time in this life to share with his son here on earth.

We never mentioned the name of the doctor I was doubting, but I'm sure that Dr. H. was able to find out easily who he was. We never cared to find out if there were changes made; it was not important to us. Our only concern was for Jake to be given the care he deserved. Now, he was. In just a couple of months after that meeting, things were in motion and the date of the surgery had been scheduled.

After almost two, long years of what I will always believe was unnecessary stress and sickness for Jake, it was now the night before the surgery and Jake was admitted to the hospital to be sure nothing would happen to delay this transplant from happening. We must remember that *life* happens. We won't always understand when there are problems and heartaches, but never forget that God is with us even when we don't realize it, and the waiting for answers seems almost too late.

> *"The Lord is close to the brokenhearted*
> *and saves those who are crushed in spirit."*
> *--Psalm 34:18 (NIV)*

This time, instead of waiting until the morning of the surgery to come to the hospital, to be sure Jason would be there on time without having to worry about getting caught in traffic, we got a couple of rooms in a hotel in Charlotte. The growth of the area had increased the traffic, reminding us of the bumper-to-bumper traffic we had left behind so many years ago in California. We were not going to take a chance of anything at all delaying this transplant from taking place.

CHAPTER 37: Celebration of Renewed Life

*"Heal me, O Lord, and I shall be healed, save
me and I shall be saved, for you are
my praise."*
--Jeremiah 17:14 (KJV)

Gary and I had one room, and Jason and his wife, Lisa, had the room next door. Gary, Lisa, and I were a little selfish that night. We knew it was going to be a long day tomorrow, and we noticed there was a *Ruth's Chris Steak House* directly across the street from our hotel. We saw it from our windows. Nothing sounded better than one of their juicy, tender steaks with all the sides and the delicious desserts available to top it all off. We couldn't resist! To us it was a place for celebrating very special occasions, so we didn't go there often, but this night we thought, *Why not?* What better reason for a celebration even though Jacob was in the hospital already, and Jason could not join us, since he was not to have anything to eat before the surgery. That really sounds super selfish now that I am writing about it!

But the three of us couldn't stop our mouths from watering, just thinking about it. Jason was really good about it all. He didn't see any reason for us not to enjoy ourselves when he knew it would be a long time tomorrow until we would be able to get a good meal.   We did not want to leave him alone, so we ordered to have it delivered. We were nice though and did not eat it in front of Jason. We went to our room to eat, so he didn't have to watch us enjoying it. After our bellies were very filled, we all settled down to try to get some rest before the early morning hour came for us to get ready and go to the hospital.

We were at the hospital before 4:30 a.m. the next morning, ahead of when we needed to be there. We checked in on Jake, and he was looking rested, relieved, and ready to get this all started. Dr. H., and the other surgeons came in and talked with us. Soon it was time for the boys to be taken and prepped, so the surgery could begin right on time.

When they were in their gowns and had their cute slippers on to keep their feet warm, the IV's hooked up to administer the anesthesia, and all the other preparations done, we were told we could go back and be with them a few minutes before it was time to take them in for the surgery.

The boys were smiling and showed no signs of being scared or worried. It took me back to the day that I was there in the bed beside Jake all those long years before. I knew they had the same peace about what was going to happen and knew all would be well. God's presence was felt by us all—Blessed Assurance!

We helped put the caps on their heads to cover their hair. They really should create fun hats to wear when going under the knife. It could be a last-minute laugh for everyone to lighten the mood. Maybe I should work on that! They were all settled and ready now. This was really going to happen. Finally! Our prayers of thanks for this day were filling our hearts.

The orderly arrived to take Jason in first, so the surgeon

who would be harvesting his left kidney could begin the process. We had our final hugs and kisses before the orderly started to push Jason's bed toward the doors. As the bed was being pushed away, all of a sudden Jason yelled, "Wait!"

It startled us! I don't know if he realized how loud he had yelled that, but the poor orderly must have thought he did something to hurt Jason by the look he had on his face. He turned and looked over at us like he didn't know what to think or do next. None of us did. We were pretty shocked and were just waiting to see what Jason was going to say next.

There was just a second when I was thinking, *Oh no! Please don't say you've changed your mind now!*

I really didn't think he would ever do that, but you do wonder what might be coming after hearing someone yell out like that. Jason turned so he could look back at Jake, who had not been moved yet. He stretched his arm toward his brother saying, "I love you, Jake." His eyes connected only with his brother's eyes. Without a second's hesitation, along with a glimmering of tears in his eyes, Jacob told his brother, the brother who had grown miraculously with him in the womb, "I love you too, Jase."

Jason smiled, turned back around, and nodded for the orderly to continue pushing him out the door toward the operating room where the surgeon was waiting to begin. There are no sweeter words for parents to hear spoken than those words between your thirty-six-year-old sons and knowing they were meant for now and always, just as God knew it would be because He had planned it all.

It was much harder being on the waiting side when two people you love are being operated on at the same time. The hours seemed like a lifetime before we knew they were doing great. Both surgeries had been a success, and the kidney began working immediately and beautifully after it was in Jake. The total time of both surgeries took about the same amount of time -- three hours each -- even with the laparoscopic method being used on Jason.

I could not imagine how tedious it must have been for the surgeon using a scope (camera) and special miniaturized surgical instruments to preform removal of a kidney through such a small cut instead of having a wide-open space to remove it. This type of surgery had required an inch incision in the lower abdomen for the kidney to be removed and four smaller incisions to serve as ports for the instruments to enter and remove the left kidney. That was definitely more tedious than having more open space to work in for sure. The steadiness of a surgeon's hands during these operations leaves me in awe. I can't even thread a needle to sew without trying over and over.

Jake's surgery was performed in the same way it had been done before, via the traditional open surgery method. His recovery would probably be a little longer with all that had happened up to the surgery, but there would be no more dialysis and no more seeing every kind of doctor every time he turned around anymore.

We were very thankful when we got the news both surgeries had gone beautifully and our sons were doing great; all was well. The ability to take a big breath of relief after such a long time of pain and sorrow overwhelmed me. I didn't have the proper words of thanks for the doctors, the nurses, and for God to express what I was feeling. Seeing goodness and hope ahead was so wonderful. Happy crying, even though it can give you a very ugly-looking face, helps you release a lot of that built up worry and can take the place of words at times! What a blessed time of rejoicing!

Jason was released to go home first and Jake not too long after. Jason got back to his active life. He has never been one to sit around for too long. He loves getting out to camp, ride his bike, and plan fun family events. Even though Jake did not have the same wonderful experience that he did with his first transplant, we are still able to be thankful that everything ended up going well, and he has a kidney that is expected to keep going for a very long time. He is here to share life with us and with his son as he grows and matures. Liam graduated from high school this year and is beginning a new chapter in his life. We are so thankful that Jake is able to be here to encourage him and be his example as he makes his way in this world.

Getting through and past the years of uncertainty and stress while Jake was so sick and we were struggling with what was going on was a challenge at the time, but it has made us all stronger in the confidence we will make it through the things that we will face.

The words from an old hymn by John H. Sammis in 1887 comes to mind. I remember singing it when I was a child. It is a perfect reminder to follow, so we can be at peace about whatever might happen in life:

"Trust and obey, for there's no other way to be happy in Jesus, but to trust and obey."

CHAPTER 38: So Unexpected

*"When Jesus spoke again to the people, he said, 'I Am the
light of the world. Whoever follows me will never walk in
darkness, but will have the light of life.'"*
--John 8:12 (NIV)

Life was moving on really well for a number of years.
Jake continued doing great, and Jason had no problems from
being the donor. All the daily routines of life continued, and
the grandkids were doing well, growing taller each year, and
making this Grammy and Grampy look shorter and shorter.
None of us expected or could even have imagined that something would happen in our world to change all of our lives,
altering the usual way we were used to living each day.

A deadly coronavirus, believed to have originated in
Wuhan, China, in late 2019, became a threat world-wide.
The elderly, those with life threatening illnesses, transplant
patients, and others who depended on life saving procedures
and medications, which included Jake with his kidney transplant, and our eldest grandson, Garrett, who had been diagnosed as a Type 1 diabetic at the age of six-years-old, became a
great concern for families to ensure they were protected from
contracting this deadly virus. Soon though, we found that
everyone was at risk, seemingly healthy people were testing
positive for the virus. It was not long before everyone realized

that life was going to be very different for a long time.

The world was not prepared for something like this at all. The virus quickly began to spread all over the world and quickly became a Global Health Emergency. In March of 2020, our then president, Donald J. Trump, declared this virus a National Emergency for the United States. The whole world would be changed dramatically in ways that most of us had never thought possible in this day and age. Month after month more and more people were testing positive for COVID-19 and deaths were mounting all over the world in heartbreaking numbers.

Very quickly it became like time was put on hold. We were told to stay in our homes, to not get out around other people in hope the spreading of this virus could slow and hopefully be prevented from spreading further, but even with all the precautions, the virus just kept spreading. Schools were shut down, churches closed their doors, businesses and restaurants shut down, movie theaters closed, and shopping malls and stores closed. Weddings and even funerals were cancelled or postponed along with everything else. The streets were eerily empty; everything was still.

Only necessary workers, like doctors and nurses, gas station attendants, and some grocery store personnel were permitted to work. No travel was allowed anywhere. All state and federal borders had been closed and airplanes and cruise ships were grounded. It was all so surreal.

The hospitals became so filled with patients that there were no spare rooms. Most scheduled surgeries were postponed. The patients diagnosed with this virus were lined up in hallways on stretchers waiting to be cared for. Doctors and nurses were so overworked trying to keep up with the demand. Families could not visit their loved ones in the hospital for fear the virus would spread further, and loved ones died alone without having any family around them. The death rate was catastrophic; truck trailers were being setup outside hospitals to hold the dead until arrangements could be made for them to be cremated or buried. There were no funeral services and family could not even attend the burials. This was not an isolated happening; the whole world was experiencing this devastation. The virus seemed unstoppable. Death was all around.

The last pandemic of this severity had happened over one hundred years before, during the 1918 influenza pandemic called ("The Spanish Flu Pandemic"). The current virus had been named ("COVID 19"). The public was scared and really didn't know what to do or expect. It did not help that there were always conflicting news reports we were hearing on television from those who were supposed to be telling us how to handle this. They were never really sure themselves. One day they would report that everyone should wear a mask, and then next they would say don't wear one; it doesn't really help. Then later we'd be told, "Yes do wear one; it is now mandatory. As time went by, we would hear that you could go out only if it is necessary. Wear a mask and stay at least six feet apart from other people. Before long, that would change. We would be told not to be with family for holidays or attend any functions where there might be crowds. There was so much confusion and uncertainty that you really didn't know what you should be doing.

Amazingly, some people didn't take the threat seriously, even after hearing about all the deaths and refused to take any precautions at all. Others thought it would be funny to spit and smear their germs over surfaces that others might have to touch in certain places. Evil always seems to find a way to make itself known even when so many are suffering and dying. Don't ever doubt the power of Satan in this world. He is always working in every way possible to turn weak people away from believing in Jesus.

It wasn't long before it was reported that there had been over 570,000 deaths in the United States and over 2,600,000 deaths worldwide. In May 2020, the Trump administration worked with pharmaceutical companies to develop a COVID-19 vaccine with the hope to find one to protect the population from a continued spread of the deathly virus. We had to do something to prevent a continued rise in deaths. Of course, like everything when sides cannot agree, much controversy and disagreements ran rampant as to how things should be handled: how to agree on a vaccine, how to distribute them, and even who would get credit for saving lives when the vaccine was developed and proven to be working.

It was July. Just two months later a vaccine was developed and clinical trials began. Reported timelines as to when the vaccine would start to be distributed to the public changed time after time, depending on who was doing the reporting. It was hard to trust or believe any of the media, and the uncertainty and frustration continued to rise. By the end of December 2020, the first vaccines began to be distributed.

In the United States, the first to receive the vaccine were healthcare workers and the elderly people who were at risk living in nursing homes. By early 2021, the vaccine was available to those who were aged seventy-five and older. Then each age group followed as more doses of the vaccines became available. As months went by, people being accepted to sign up to get their shot would include younger and younger ages. The United States was doing a good job trying to get everyone vaccinated who wanted it. Some vaccines had to be destroyed because they were not handled safely, and some countries could and still cannot get enough for everyone. The cases of those testing positive lowered one month, then rose the next.

Unfortunately, in mid 2021, we were hearing more about a second wave of COVID-19, called the Delta variant that was spreading again. I fully expected to see more changes beginning to happen. Most of us who had gotten the vaccine had not been wearing masks because we were told the vaccine would protect us, but then we were hearing some who had the vaccine were still getting COVID. I was concerned and ready to begin wearing masks again and avoiding certain crowded places. I prayed it didn't get as bad as it was before. We were finally beginning to act *normal* again: attending church, eating out in restaurants, and being with family and friends again. There is no certainty about when or if things will return to how they were before this virus began.

As I write this book, some people are still working from home and have not returned to their workplace. Some countries have opened their borders for travel and others have not. And some who had opened them are considering closing them again. Only time will tell what life will be like in the future. The past two years have certainly been hard for many people in so many different ways. Not only those getting sick, but those who have lost their jobs, lost their homes, and / or lost hope. It has been such a troubling time, a time of devastation and division. It has not been a time of coming together and wanting the best for others like you saw during times when there was a hurricane, for example. Instead, I am seeing more hatred for one another, more taking than giving, and more self-entitlement than I have ever seen before. It is troubling that people seem to have forgotten the love of God and how we are taught to treat each other with love. The message needs to be heard and listened to and lived, or there is going to be a lot of hard times for many people who don't realize they are heading for a very dark eternity.

Reflecting on all of this, I feel now more strongly than before that I have a responsibility to share, as a mother and a grandmother, by taking this opportunity to write this book and to live a life that helps change those full of hatred to become full of love instead. I hope to be an avenue to help others to accept Jesus into their lives and follow the word of God by sharing His love for one another instead of spreading hatred during their lifetimes.

I am not a preacher, not even a college-educated teacher. I am just me. You can call me Grammy. I'm writing from my heart because I want a life filled with love, happiness, joy, blessings, and all goodness for everyone. It is available for everyone, and it is a wonderful way to live. I promise it is better than the opposite way of living a life of hatred, sorrow, hopelessness, and misery.

When you finish reading the rest of this book, it does not matter if you remember my name. The only name that is important to remember after reading this story is the name of Jesus, the son of God. Jesus will show you the way to live in love, and His name is the name to keep forever in your mind and your heart.

> *"Search me, O God, and know my heart; test*
> *me and know my anxious thoughts. See if*
> *there is any offensive way in me, and lead me*
> *in the everlasting way."*
> *--Psalm 138:23-24*

CHAPTER 39: Given for Us All

"If you declare with your mouth, 'Jesus is
Lord' and believe in your heart that God
raised him from the dead, you will be saved."
--Romans 10:9 (NIV)

Sadly, I have watched as others, who have not fully accepted and obeyed the Word of God, live a life without knowing joy and having faith they will be in Heaven when they die. It must be awful to be afraid to die. Death is a new beginning to a life more wonderful than we can ever imagine. I could not bear to leave this world without knowing I have done my best to help others to believe in Jesus and have no doubt of the eternal life in Heaven that is available to those who do believe. It is heartbreaking when they choose not to accept Jesus into their heart.

Jesus has already done the hard part for us. All that is asked of us is to do what is required as instructed in the Bible, the Word of God, to show we really want to be in Heaven with Him after our life here is finished. There are no hard activities required of us -- no pain and torture. Jesus took that upon himself -- more pain and torture than we can ever imagine. He paid the price for our sins, and He did it for you and me. The steps are clearly written in the Bible for us to read. We are to learn and follow what is written and be obedient to what we are told.

You can think of it like being in school, learning in a

class that will help you decide what type of work you want to do to make your life a good one and be able to provide for yourself and your family to the best of your ability. In all learning, you need to read or listen and learn what to do. You have to follow the instructions to be able to receive something that will make things better for you. The wonderful thing about learning the lessons in the Bible is that if you are obedient to what you learn and always believe in what it tells you, your reward will be like no other. It will be something better than you can even imagine.

We all want to get a good grade and do not want to fail the class. The only way you can fail after learning what you read in the Bible about eternal life is by choosing to ignore it all and turn away from Jesus -- turning away from the One Who is the light of the world and following Satan, who is the darkness.

It is your choice whom you will follow; the two options are light or darkness. You can choose a life in eternity with Jesus or a death in Hell with Satan. I choose the light; I pray you do, too.

Allow me to take you through the steps that Jesus made so simple for us to follow in words that may be easier to understand than if I just gave you the chapters and verses to read in the Bible yourself. By following these steps, you will know it will be the best thing you have been obedient to in your entire life.

The first step to choosing Jesus is to acknowledge that we are sinners. We have to realize that and not deny we do things that are wrong. We all sin. We are not perfect, and we all do things we know are wrong for us and for others. We know when we are doing something wrong, but sometimes we choose to make excuses for it or choose to ignore that it is wrong. We are required to confess our sins. If we deny our sins, we are separating ourselves from God and His goodness that He wants us to receive in our lives.

Many people pray and then they say, "God never answers my prayers. I pray all the time, and I never see anything change or get better." That is because we are not connected to Him because of our sin. He cannot look upon sin. We must confess our sin and ask for forgiveness first.

When we obey His word, we can be forgiven, and then He will hear our prayers. He may not answer them the way we want, but He will answer in the way that is best for us. Sometimes we pray selfish prayers. We tell God what we want. We don't pray that His will be done in our lives. Instead, we tell Him how we want things done. That is not prayer; that is making demands.

We need to follow the instructions that we are given in the Bible. We need a relationship with Jesus Who is our connection to God, so we will be heard in our times of need. Until we do that, our prayers are as if *falling on deaf ears*. After acknowledging that we are sinners, the next steps are easy. We need to **Hear the Word, Believe It, Repent of Our Sins, and Confess Our Belief in Jesus Christ by Being Baptized.**

So now, after we have quit denying we are sinning, we will then need to hear the word, study it, and become familiar with its teachings. The word was spoken by God and recorded by men into the sixty-six books that we know as the Bible. Every circumstance that has ever or will ever happen and how we are to handle them has been recorded for us to read about.

Everything we can think of is addressed, and we are told how we are to live our life in a way that is pleasing to God. Our example is the way Jesus lived His life when He was on this earth. He was without sin. Even when tempted by the devil, He obeyed God's word. We, ourselves, can now freely read and learn from events that began taking place over more than four hundred thousand years ago. *The Dead Sea Scrolls* have been discovered showing transcripts recorded of some of these books in the Bible.

Gary and I have been blessed to travel to Israel and see the site where some of the scrolls were found. We have seen pieces of the parchments that the Hebrew and Greek words were recorded onto when an exhibit was in Charlotte, North Carolina, years ago. The proof of God's Word is there to be seen and cannot be denied.

The Bible is the most fascinating book we will ever read and has everything from romance to murder in it. The best part of the Bible is that no other book we could ever read or listen to ends by promising good (love) wins over evil (hate) for eternity. If we choose the right path during our journey here on earth, we will live in eternity in the presence of Jesus in a place that is more spectacular than we can even imagine or explain. It is beyond our comprehension in the most glorious way.

Even though I cannot comprehend what it will really be like, what I do know and have every confidence about is the Bible reveals enough for me to know that I want to spend eternity in Heaven, not in Hell. Scripture says that there will be no night (darkness), no fear, no suffering, and no death. All the pain and disabilities and diseases of every kind we face in this life will be gone. We will have new glorified bodies, and Jesus will walk among us there.

The only other place to spend eternity is Hell, which is being forever separated from God. We have all heard the word *hell* and usually when we do it is associated with things that are not good or positive. Some of the ways it is described is that it is like a garbage dump, a prison, an unquenchable fire, a place of great pain, torture and suffering the worst of anything you can imagine, and as the ultimate darkness with no escaping it, *ever!*

In order to hear the Word, we can, of course, read the books of the Bible, thus we are hearing it in our mind and retaining it in our memory. There are many other ways to hear the Word of God. We can listen to it on our radio or a podcast or watch television, or watch a video.

Attending church services where the messages are taught from the Bible is always a great way to hear the Word of God. Also, being around other people who are reading and studying and then discussingwith each other what was read is a wonderful way to learn through fellowship with others. And one of my favorite ways to hear the word of God is to listen to Christian music and hear about the goodness of our God being shared in songs.

Christian music comes in all genres. If you are not a listener of Christian music, you may think that it is all like the old hymns of long ago, and those wonderful hymns tell beautiful stories of the love of God for us. But if you think those are just too old fashioned for you to listen to then you might be surprised to know that Christian music is shared in songs through every kind of music now. Artists who sing hiphop, rock, metal, contemporary Christian, country, blues, and even rap also sing Christian songs now. Even Snoop Dog has a great Christian song out there entitled "Grateful" that shares a wonderful message of hope and love. There is something for everyone out there no matter what type of music you like. It is important to listen to the words of the song in all music, to really listen to the words and hear what they are telling us about the goodness and love of Jesus and how to live as a good example to others. Whatever way you choose to hear and listen to the teachings from God, you will be filling your mind with good instead of evil, hope instead of hopelessness. Music like this will make you happy and will lead to finding comfort and peace in your life.

BELIEVING what you hear will be a natural step for you when you are consistent with your hearing and learning more about Jesus. You will start to store it in your sub-conscious and more than likely start singing along with the songs you enjoy. The messages in the songs that begin to fill your mind will change your attitude about how you handle events in your life. You will see more of the positive side of everything, instead of always dwelling on the negative you were letting happen before. You will realize that you were allowing lies about yourself and others to control your thoughts and actions, causing you to feel hopeless and miserable.

As hope and happiness take control, you will begin to find that life can be so much better than it was in the past. This new outlook opens the way to the next step, one you will be ready to obey. This next act of obedience will be to REPENT. To repent means to feel and express sincere regret or remorse for things you have done wrong: your sins.

Repenting leads you to making a change in your life, turning from the old ways of how you lived before and making the decision to commit to changing the direction of your life by turning to Jesus, living by His example, and being obedient to God in all things. Be a good person in every way, pleasing to God, instead of being an evil person, pleasing Satan.

"A good man brings good things out of the good stored up in his heart, and an evil man brings evil things out of the evil stored up in his heart. For the mouth speaks what the heart is full of."
--Luke 6:45 (NIV)

This verse from Luke speaks to truth. What you hear and store in your mind and heart is what you will be. Just think about it. You are choosing what you read, what you listen to, who you choose to be around, how you treat others, and the attitude you have toward everything. You alone are making those choices; it is what defines you. Yes, others can treat you wrong, hurt you, disappoint you, but it is up to you to make the decision on how you will let those things affect you. This is why you need Jesus; without Him, you will make the wrong decisions about how you will react.

When you choose to live differently, you will begin to realize that with all the struggles and hard times so far in your life, you have not been able to make things seem better on your own so far and that following the way of the world (the way of darkness and sin) has not made it any better. Your eyes are being opened to seeing that you need Jesus in your life to make it better. By realizing this need and wanting to change, you are *maturing* in the Word. You will notice a change in how you are feeling: not getting as upset as you used to when things went wrong, being calmer, and handling your temper and your hateful attitude toward others. Not only will you begin to notice this change in yourself, but others will notice it too. Those you know will probably comment on how you seem calmer and are not getting as upset and losing control of your emotions when things go wrong. Not only that, but your Heavenly Father has noticed it all along, and He is rejoicing because you are ready to receive the good that He wants to provide for you in your life while living on earth and the promise of eternity in Heaven.

The last step required for you to have every confidence that you will receive this promise that God is freely offering to you through His son, Jesus, is to be BAPTIZED. The Greek word for baptism is *Baptizo,* which means immersed. I believe that immersion is what we are being asked to fulfill as believers in Jesus Christ. This obedient act of being baptized is symbolic. You enter the water and stand, waiting to be immersed. This standing and waiting is symbolic of Jesus dying on the cross. The act of being lowered into the water symbolizes Jesus being buried in the tomb; being raised up from the water symbolizes Jesus rising from the dead. After being raised up from the body of water, you are declaring to others that you have accepted Jesus into your life and are being raised with Him into a brand-new life being baptized in the name of The Father (God), The Son (Jesus), and the Holy Ghost (the Spirit of God).

Jesus Christ was baptized in the Jordan River in an

area outside of Jerusalem called Qasr el Yahud, north of the Dead Sea. His being baptized marked the beginning of His public ministry. When he came up out of the water, Heaven opened and the spirit of God descended like a dove on him. God from Heaven said, *"This is my Son, whom I love, with Him I am well pleased"* (Matthew 3:17, NIV).

Then Jesus was led by the Holy Spirit into the Judean Desert. He fasted forty days and forty nights and then was tempted by the devil (Satan) when he was weak and hungry. The devil tempted him many times, trying to get him to deny God and worship him instead. The devil promised him riches, and kingdoms, and to save him from all the torture he would have to face if he stayed true to God, His father. Jesus never turned from God; He never sinned; He remained faithful and steadfast to what is good, and He followed all the instructions required of Him to make it possible for us to be forgiven for our sins.

The Holy Spirit enters into us and remains with us as our helper when we falter and start slipping into the darkness. He never leaves us when we believe in Him and keep our faith. While Jesus lived as man on this earth, He was beaten, had undergone rejection by his closest friends, and had no sleep. He was arrested and forced to walk miles and miles to be taken to court where He would be judged and condemned after being betrayed.

He was condemned to be put to death by crucifixion by the evil people who did not believe that He was the Son of God, the Messiah, as was being proclaimed by those who knew him. Dying by crucifixion was the most horrible death ever. The Romans used this gruesome mode of execution to control and intimidate whoever they decided to accuse of a crime, so they could put to death those who would interfere with what they wanted. Crucifixion was sometimes used by emperors as a type of amusement. Only followers of Satan could watch something as horrific as this and consider it entertainment for them to enjoy.

Let me describe to you the accounts of death by crucifixion that took place upon the cross when Jesus paid the price for our sins. I will paraphrase what I've learned in church worship services, *Passion of the Christ,* and in an article, "Crucifixion Details of the Resurrection of Christ" by John McDowell Ministry. I pray that you will be truly thankful with all your heart for His suffering on our account, realizing the sacrifice of God's only Son as the price paid for us, so we can be forgiven of our sins and be in His presence in eternity. God's love allowed all this, so we will not have to be in all the pain and torture that there will be for those who don't accept Jesus into their lives and believe in Him.

We all can imagine and fear things like electrocution, drowning, being burnt alive, and other possible causes of death and how horrible those would be for us to have to experience before our physical bodies could no longer function. Crucifixion was even more horrific than any type of painful death we could imagine. It was a type of execution that the Romans spent much time *perfecting*. As I mentioned earlier, they were evil and wanted to make it the worst kind of death ever for the people they wanted to make an example of to show what would happen if the people did not obey what they demanded them to do or spoke against those in charge.

Jesus was tortured even before he was nailed to the cross. He was mocked, humiliated, stripped of his clothing, and, then after having his hands tied to a post above his head, He was flogged. The flogging was done to his bare body by being whipped across His shoulders, back, buttocks, thighs, and legs, bringing Him right to the brink of death. Only then would the flogging stop because they did not want Him to die yet. They were not finished inflicting all the pain they wanted to do before letting Him actually be free in death.

The whips used to flog him, which were called *flagrums* (scourge), were short heavy leather thongs (straps) with sharp pieces of lead, bone, or iron (like shrapnel) attached near the end of each one. Many times, pieces of sheep's jagged bones were included with the iron and lead to cause deeper cuts and more pain. The wounds of the torn flesh continued to get wider and deeper with each strike of the whip. Severe bleeding occurs because capillaries and veins were cut along with arteries and muscle. Jesus was at the point of collapse when He was cut down from the flogging-post.

They covered Him with a cloth, allowing the blood to dry into the fabric, only later to rip the cloth from His skin and pulling the wounds open again, which caused more pain for Him to endure. This was just the beginning of the pain Jesus endured for our sake.

Evil and corrupt people (unbelievers) demanded that He be crucified. They made a crown from twisted bands with long thorns and drove it down onto his head, causing profuse bleeding. They forced Him to carry the crossbar of the cross on his beaten and bloody shoulders while walking through the winding, uneven cobblestone streets of Jerusalem to the out side of the city walls where the upright post had been placed in the ground for the crossbar to be attached for Him to hang for His crucifixion. This was the place called Golgotha, the *Place of the Skull*, (Calvary).

The streets that Jesus walked along came to be called the *Via Delarosa (Via Dolorosa)*, which is Latin for *Sorrowful Way*, often called *Way of Suffering*, and *Way of Pain*. The route goes through the old city of Jerusalem and is marked by nine *Stations of the Cross* along the path. It is not just one street, but segments of many streets, converging from different directions along the way.

It was a long and hard walk for Jesus as He was close to death and being forced to carry the cross bar on His shoulders. He was suffering every step of the way, stumbling, and falling many times as He was forced on by the Roman soldiers until He could no longer stand. When they arrived outside the city to where Jesus would be hung, the Roman soldiers threw him down on his back and stretched His arms out along the crossbar and then drove nails through His wrists into the wood. These nails were not like nails you are picturing; they were iron spikes about 6 inches long and 3/8 inches thick. When they were driven into his wrist, they cut the large nerve in His wrist causing excruciating pain in his arms. The nails were placed between the bones and ligaments of the wrist to be able to bear the full weight of a man being crucified. The Romans wanted to ensure Jesus didn't die quickly. They wanted to ensure they could inflict more pain and suffering before His body could no longer stand any more of the torture before causing His heart to stop.

After the crossbar was in place on the post, His legs

were bent at the knees, and the same type of nails were driven into each ankle, nailing his feet to the cross and causing the same severe nerve damage and intense pain in His legs as He experienced in His arms.

Because of the precise placement of the nails through his wrists and ankles, there was not a lot of bleeding from these wounds.That was not done out of sympathy for Jesus; it was done with the specific intention to make sure no major arteries would rupture in order to ensure death would indeed be slower and the suffering longer like everything else the Romans had done to ensure the most pain possible. If a major artery had been ruptured, death would have been faster because of the quick loss of blood from the heart. That would be a disappointment to the evil Romans after they had spent so much time perfecting their craft of death by crucifixion.

The reason for the wrist and ankles being nailed as they were was the cruel way of ensuring agonizing pain for those who were to be crucified. Already being so weak and close to death, a person's body would be sagging downward, making it hard to breath. The Roman's bent the knees of those they were crucifying so that when they tried to push themselves up to take a breath, the pain in their legs and feet would become unbearable, and they would then try to pull themselves up using their shoulders to straighten enough to take a breath. This struggle of trying to push and pull their body up and down was also causing more pain as their raw and bloody back from being flogged was being scraped and filled with splinters from the rough wood of the post of the cross. Eventually, from all the strain and struggle of the weight trying to lift up, their shoulders would be pulled out of the sockets, leaving them without a way to get air into their lungs to breathe.

Can you think of anything that could be more horrible than this constant pain and suffering and agonizing torture? The accused knew he was going to die but fought with whatever little strength he had to keep breathing. I imagine this is just a tiny glimpse of what eternity in Hell must be like.

The fact that Hell is a total, conscious, eternal separation from God is enough for me not to want to end up there. For those who do not accept Jesus and continue to follow the evil of the world, along with what I believe might be just a glimpse of Hell, the Bible further describes those who are condemned to eternity in Hell will have the constant pain of being lashed as stung by scorpions. They will be in the realm of darkness where there is a constant binding or grinding (gnashing) of teeth in a place of extreme torment by being where the fire that burns, the eternal lake of fire, will not be quenched. And this is forever for those who choose not to love the Lord our God with all our hearts, souls, and minds. Jesus was sent to save us all from that eternal punishment.

After all He had endured up to this time, Jesus suffered on the cross for hours. Then when His heart could no longer beat, He cried out with a loud voice, *"Father, into your hands I commit my spirit" and died (Luke 23:46, NIV).* He had finished what God, His Father, sent Him to earth to do: to teach the Gospel (the Word of God), to perform miracles, proving He was the son of God, and to achieve reconciliation for all who believe in Him. He paid the ultimate price, so we can be forgiven. The price of betrayal was humiliation, pain, torture, and death by crucifixion. He obeyed God who loves us so much that He sent His only Son, Jesus, to take all that upon

Himself, so we can be able to ask for forgiveness for our sins.

Pause for a moment and really take all of this in? Really think about it and try to comprehend all that happened to Jesus while He lived as a man on this earth. He could have refused. He could have turned from God and turned to Satan to *save* Himself and not have to bear the pain and torture for the sins of the world.

He could have said, "Too bad all you people; you can just spend eternity in Hell if you don't want to believe in God." But He didn't. He loved us that much!

How can we not obey the simple request to turn to the good, to leave the evil behind, and to accept Jesus into our lives after what He did for you and me? I am thankful every minute of my life that I am loved that much.

"Whoever believes in the Son (Jesus) has
eternal life, But whoever rejects the Son will not see
life, for God's Wrath remains on them."
–John 3:36 (NIV)

"Know therefore that the LORD your God is
God; he is the faithful God, keeping his
covenant of love to a thousand generations of those
who love him and keep his commandments."
--Deuteronomy 7:9 (NIV)

"But because of his great love for us, God, who is rich in mercy, made us alive with Christ even when we were dead in our transgressions – it is by grace you have been saved."
--Ephesians 2:4-5 (NIV)

Gary and me getting baptized in the Jordan River.

CHAPTER 40: Encouragement and Help

"Do not let any unwholesome talk come out
of your mouths, but only what is helpful for
building others up according to their needs,
that it may benefit those who listen."
--Ephesians 4:29 (NIV)

There is always more for all of us to learn about the life of Jesus and all that took place before He came to pay the price for our sins. I encourage you to seek help to be able to understand the Word more clearly. If you don't own a Bible, take time to look at different translations and choose one that is easy for you to read. There is even a Children's Bible that is excellent if you are brand new to studying the Bible.

Let me share a few translations here to show you some options that are available. There are many translations, maybe too many actually, but you will discover one you will enjoy reading and are able to understand as you become familiar with the different versions. I recommend the NIV (New International Version) or the NLT (New Living Translation) if you are new to the Bible. The KJV (King James Version) is one you will want to eventually read and compare with the others, but at first, it might be hard to understand.

The KJV was published in 1611 after being translated from the original Hebrew and Greek languages. It is still widely used and good for referring back to when studying as you mature in reading and understanding the Word.

Below you will read a verse I chose to share, which shows the ways different versions are written. The first translation is from the NIV or New International Version. The second translation is from the NLT or New Living Translation. The final translation is from the KJV or King James Version. The Bible verse I am sharing for you to compare is found in the New Testament (the second half of the Bible). This scripture is from the second book of Timothy, in chapter 3, verses 16 and 17. This is normally written as 2 Timothy 3:16-17.

The NIV Version: *"All Scripture is God-breathed and is useful for teaching, rebuking, correcting and training in righteousness, so that the servant of God may be thoroughly equipped for every good work."*

The NLT Version: *"All Scripture is inspired and is useful to teach us what is true and to make us realize the wrong things we are doing in our life. It guides us on how to correct the wrong ways we are living so that we can receive the grace and mercy promised to us through Jesus Christ by God."*

The KJV Version: *"All Scripture is given by inspiration of God, and is profitable for doctrine, for reproof, for correction, for instruction in righteousness: That the man of God be perfect, thoroughly furnished unto all good works."*

This example illustrates three versions and how they read differently. The message is the same in each of the versions, but you may find it easier to understand one of the different versions than another one. I like to compare versions when I am studying. I also like to read Bible-based study guides to help when things are not clear to me. I was given a great study source back in 1975 called the *Halley's Bible Handbook*. It helped to make it easier for me to understand certain verses in the Bible I was having trouble with. Even at my age, there is always something new to understand more clearly and open my eyes to the meaning of what has been written. There is a newer version of this handbook out now that I just ordered, and I would recommend that you might want one to help you when you are reading and studying the Bible, too.

If you do not have a Bible, the Internet is a great way to read it and compare how different versions are written. Or if you enjoy actually going to bookstores like I do, take time to look at the different versions available there. Might I be so bold as to challenge you to spend a little time each day reading just a chapter or part of a chapter to begin your journey of reading and hearing the Word of God. Just be sure to read in context; don't stop in the middle of something and not get the complete message you are reading about. For example, the first day read John, chapter 1, verses 1 to 28. The next day read the remainder of chapter 1, instead of stopping halfway between verses 1 and 28 -- just reading part of what is written. The Gospel of John is the fourth book found in the New Testament and is a good place to begin to understand who Jesus is and to learn more about what He did for us.

I do not recommend you pick up a Bible and start reading the Old Testament first. That will just confuse you, as it did me, and still does at times. When you read more and more of the Bible, you will see that the Old Testament will be something you will want to eventually refer back to so you can see that things happening in the New Testament were foretold about in the Old Testament, validating they were of God. I promise the Bible is the best book ever written.

I do love music, and there are amazing Christian songs from every genre out there to listen to as I mentioned previously. Yes, there are still the ones you might consider old-fashion and you may want to listen to them again one day, but start out searching for songs in the genre you like and give them a try. Most of the songs have great videos that you can watch that show a story that can make the message more real to you. I don't have to instruct you on how to listen to music or watch music videos. Just look up contemporary Christian songs and go for it. Like all songs, the ones that have been listened to the most are good ones to start listening to first. Then branch out from there.

Again, let me challenge you to listen to one or two a day. Some singers you might enjoy are *Crowder, Zack Williams, Andrew Ripp, King & Country, Toby Mac, Colton Dixon, and Need to Breath,* just to name a few. I do not want to overwhelm you by listing all I enjoy here, but I will list more in the back of the book that you might want to check out too. I know you will find some songs you will really like and can explore more of the songs by those artists to listen to and learn the words of, so you can sing along. Some will even make you want to tap your feet as you are listening to them or maybe even get up and dance if you want to.

Get up and dance and let yourself be filled with joy. I know one reason I am usually happy and in a good mood is because music is in my head all the time. I listen when I am cleaning the house, while I am cooking dinner, when I do the laundry, and when I am writing. When I don't actually listen to it, I am replaying certain ones in my head. There is no room for bad things to enter my thoughts. And yes, I tap my feet and dance once in a while too. Grammy likes to dance!! Grampy and I used to be pretty good at *cutting the rug* as they say. I feel like I need to insert an emoji here, but I will let your imagination just work here instead.

It really is wonderful how easy it is to change our way of thinking and our attitude about things that happen in our lives once we just make the decision to do that. Most people don't think twice about buying *things* that make them feel better or buying this gadget or new thing that comes out promising to make us feel and look better. We all have done it, and we discover most of the time, those things do not work as they claim. It seems like every month now something new that guarantees it will change your life in some way is introduced. There are some dishonest motivational speakers who charge lots of money for you to go listen to them and then urge you to purchase their books and videos with promises that your life can be changed for the better if you only purchase what they are offering. Promises are spoken so casually in our day and age. More casual promises are broken than actually kept, and many are even spoken with no intent at all to keep them.

There are some speakers who are helping out of love, not out of money. You will learn to recognize and be able to trust them as you grow in your faith and knowledge. I am not talking about those writers and speakers, so don't think

I am criticizing them. I am talking about those who are not speaking the truth and are only interested in their own gain. Do your research, make sure they are reliable, and learn to trust people before spending lots of money supporting false teaching and promises.

I can with all certainty tell you of the one promise that is kept and is true, and it does not cost lots of money to learn about it. That is, of course, the promise we read about in the Bible from the Lord our God. When we believe in Jesus, we believe in God and the Holy Spirit. When we put Him first in in all things, what is promised will come to pass. God is not a liar.

The liar in the Bible is Satan, the devil as he is depicted in cartoon-like ways with horns coming out of the top of his head, carrying a pitchfork, all red and evil looking, and representing all that is deceiving and filled with hate; but in reality, he makes himself very appealing in every way. He never stops trying to persuade you to turn from God by using temptations that seem so good but will only lead to what is bad.

Satan originally was an angelic being living with God and was called Lucifer, which meant "morning star." He allowed his heart to become proud and began to think of himself as the most beautiful, most intelligent, and most powerful of all, thinking he was better than God. He desired for himself the honor and glory that belongs to God alone. He chose to rebel against God and originated, through his free will, sin and evil. He was then judged by God and banished from living in Heaven; there is no sin or evil in Heaven. His name was changed to Satan, meaning *adversary* and he has never stopped spreading sin and evil in every way he can, trying to get us to turn away from God and follow him. He wants us to be in Hell with him for eternity -- in the lake of fire.

He desires his kingdom of evil to be bigger than God's heavenly kingdom. I pray you will not be tricked to suffer for eternity.

The bottom line here is that *it is all your choice!* God does not force you. He lets you make the decision to accept or reject what He offers, just as Lucifer made his own choice -- the choice to be evil instead of good. Then he was cast out of Heaven to become the enemy, trying in every way he can to make us as evil as he is so he can keep you from being a child of God. The choice is simple: It is one or the other; there is no other option.

Choose Jesus and learn to live a life filled with love, light, joy, and happiness. Choose the way to have God on your side, always with you to see you through whatever you have to face, being an ever-present help in your time of need. Learn how to be thankful, even through the storms of life. Praise God for all He has done for you and for the eternal life in glory that is promised to you when you love Him. God is the Way, the Truth, and the Life. If you don't choose Jesus, you are rejecting Jesus and God and all of His promises. This means you have chosen to follow Satan. You are following the enemy, God's adversary. Your life will be filled with hate, darkness, sadness, and unhappiness. Your life will be filled with uncertainty and confusion, blaming and cursing others. What you will have to look forward to is Hell with pain and torture leading to an eternity cast into the lake of fire with Satan, the Devil, forever. There will be no turning back if that is your choice.

Life is what you make it. It took me longer than I wished it had to really get to this point of complete peace knowing that I have this assurance and am able to know that even when things seem tough, even when they seem unfair, even when I die and am no longer here, all of it will be worth the trails and hard times I may have faced because my reward is in Heaven, and life there will be wonderful. I wish that for everyone.

I have felt an urgency to write this book for all who might read it in hopes they will be led to accept Jesus Christ into their lives and share the love of God with others, giving all glory to God.

In the book of Colossians 3:14-15 (NIV) we are instructed to set our mind on things above (Heaven), not on things of the earth (World). To keep our minds on the things of God -- what is good and shows love -- not on the sins of the world -- what is bad and produces hate.

"Above all, clothe yourselves with love which binds us all together in perfect harmony. And let the peace that comes from Christ rule in your hearts. For as members of one body, you are called to live in peace. And always be thankful."

This book is not a *goodbye book* for my children and grandchildren, not at all. I just wanted to share with them what I feel in my heart and have learned as I grow older, and with all who read it. I believe that I still have many good years left before my life comes to an end here on this earth. I hope to have many more years, so I will be able to see my grandchildren become wonderful adults -- adults who always love the Lord and raise their children in the same way. I hope to be able to watch them walk down the aisle with the right person and have children one day, so I will have the privilege of welcoming great-grandchildren into my arms. God's love has allowed me to have more love to share with more family, and I look forward to those beautiful times ahead -- more time to share the love of God.

"We love because He first loved us."
--1 John 4:19 (NIV)

Our wonderful children: Jason, Lori, Jacob

Our beautiful daughter, Lori.

Our handsome son, Jacob.

Our handsome son, Jason, and his beautiful wife, Lisa.

A Personal Note for My Grandchildren

Being a parent is not always easy, but remember that parents do the best they know how at the time. Mistakes are made; there are regrets. Looking back, we wish we could have done some things differently. We succeed in some things, and in others, we fail. We are only human, but we never stop trying to do what we can for our children. Most of us count on the promise we read in the Bible in Proverbs 22: 6 saying, *"Train up a child in the way he should go, and even when he is old, he will not depart from it" (NIV).*

As parents we fail our children when we do not stay consistent when encouraging them to continue attending church or being involved in a Bible study group with others when they get out on their own. There might be a time when they go through a period of rebellion against their parents or against authority of some kind. They may get mad at the world and may get lost along their path as they grow older. They may be having a hard time figuring out what to do and experience a feeling of hopelessness.

Parents also go through times when they feel hopeless. Those are usually the times when we don't know how to fix things for our children -- when they are going through a rough time in their lives. We feel frustrated and sometimes give up for a while. That is when we, as parents, fail our children. We need to keep an open door for communication to remind them we are always there to talk to and listen to their struggles. We need to be patient and understanding and not accuse or show anger to them when they are confused, hurting, or unsure about what is happening and why. We need to always pray for our children through every walk of their lives, so they will always find their way back to trusting in Jesus when they are led astray. And above all, we need to encourage them to pray and seek God's will for their lives.

As they get older, it is even more important to ensure they understand the importance of living their life for the Lord. I look back and see that Gary and I failed to take more time in talking with our children about how important it is to choose a husband or wife who also loves the Lord and wants to be known as a couple who wants to serve the Lord together. I guess we took it for granted they would just see that, but we did fail by not talking about it more with them.

I want to share, especially with my grandchildren, in writing some things that I have learned along the way about getting married so they will choose the right partner by seeking love through Christ. The first thing is to know that married life can be hard at times and requires a lot of effort from both the husband and the wife. It is so important to start a marriage realizing that the vows you say to each other are being promised in God's presence, and He is blessing your union as man and wife. Have a Christ-centered relationship, so when things go wrong, you will be able to go to each other and talk instead of pulling away from each other.

All married couples have times when they are annoyed and frustrated with each other. There will be times when things seem too hard, and you want to blame each other for the tough times. But with God as your foundation, you need to remember to pause, take a moment to calm down, and remember your vows and how much you love each other. You need to respect each other and talk things over to understand where each other is coming from and work it out. Encourage each other and pray for guidance. Your words and actions need to be motivated by love -- not by anger.

Most young couples spend lots of time discussing where they will get married, where the reception will take place, and where they will travel for the honeymoon. They want to be married in a church that is beautiful so their wedding photos will turn out just perfectly. They spend time and lots of money on the right venue for the reception, so it is the best party ever, and so all who attend will talk about how great it was. Of course, they want a honeymoon they can tell everyone about and share all they saw and experienced while they were there. There is nothing wrong with that, not at all, IF they know what is really important in their union as man and wife. They should have discussed and accepted the union of marriage as a holy one. They should be committed to making it a lasting one as they promised each other in the name of God.

It is right to be excited about their big day, but there are other, more important things that should have already been discussed before planning the actual wedding day. Making sure you are both Christians and want the way you live to reflect to all who you know and meet is the most important discussion you should have with the person you plan to marry. It is also important to talk about how you will handle any difficult and uncertain times that will happen after the honeymoon period is over. This is being mature and showing you are both willing to work together in a loving way to handle whatever comes your way.

Most new married couples start out madly in love. They want to do all they can for each other to make him/her happy. They don't argue much at the beginning; everything is about love. It is all wedded bliss, a real live fairy tale for them. If they have not done the real preparation for their marriage, it won't stay this way long. Real life begins to happen all around them, and unfortunately as the cliché goes, "Before you know it, the honeymoon is over."

Jobs may change, the car might break down, so stress and frustration happen. The couple may begin to realize they can't buy or have the things they thought they could for one reason or another. They want to prove they have the perfect house, car, job, and spouse to the world, but when it doesn't work out as quick as they wanted, the blame game begins to happen. It always becomes the other's fault for what has happened or why they can't have what they want when they want it.

When they start to have children and there is more responsibility for each of them, arguments about who does the most and, "Why can't you help more" begin. Arguments about how to raise the children may occur because each has his/her own way of correcting them or teaching them. This causes tension and stress. Disagreements can start over the most stupid things, such as "I want decaf coffee, and you don't!" Really! It will happen. When things begin to happen and continue to escalate instead of having a calm conversation and sharing truthfully what is bothering each other, the storm inside keeps building, and the love that was there in the beginning is forgotten. The anger begins to take over, usually resulting in a blowup with one walking out because he/she doesn't want to discuss it. That never, ever accomplishes anything for the good. The one left behind gets even more angry and upset because they are left there to handle it on their own; the one that storms out is stubborn and refuses to admit any wrong on their part and is not about to come crawling back and ask for forgiveness.

Instead of having a heart filled with love, they are allowing pride to take over. Many times, it just gets worse and worse until hatred and resentment enter the picture. Then they decide to just call it quits. They get the distorted idea they can get out and find someone with whom to have a better life, only to discover later it all seems to be happening again with the new person they found to marry. Oh, what tangled webs can be woven when love is lost.

The truth is if a marriage is not started out with being able to discuss life and how you will handle things with love when the going gets tough, it will be an unhappy marriage, things will continue to snowball into a repeat performance, and the same things will happen again and again if that commitment and strong foundation are not there from the beginning. There has to be compromise; there has to be a willingness to give and take in different circumstances; and, there has to be open discussions about each other's feelings. Don't let your commitment to each other on your wedding day get lost along the way.

A marriage must begin with a strong belief in God and a vow to love each other through *everything*. **I Corinthians 13:4-7** (NIV) needs to be studied and taken to heart when thinking about getting married. Read this verse and use it as your guide to discuss with your future spouse how your marriage should be and pray about wanting it for your life together always.

> *"Love is patient, love is kind,*
> *It does not boast,*
> *It is not proud,*
> *It does not dishonor others,*
> *It is not self-seeking,*
> *It is not easily angered,*
> *It keeps no record of wrongs.*
> *Love does not delight in evil,*
> *But rejoices with the truth.*
> *It always protects,*
> *Always hopes, always perseveres.*
> *Love never fails."*

Really, really read and comprehend what this verse is saying. Take it to heart and let it be a constant reminder to you in all walks of life.

It is not just a bunch of nice words put together to make a lightstatement. It is the way you are to live this life of yours. When you live this way, all is good, all is happy, all is right. Put others before yourselves and love and respect them, then in return you will be treated with love and respect. You will be pleasing your Heavenly Father when you express love in everything you do and you will be blessed to hear Him say to you one day, *"Well done my good and faithful servant."*

If you want to understand how easily love can be destroyed, read 1 Corinthians 13:4-7 in reverse by changing the positive to the negative. Where it says *love is*, read it as *love is not*, and where it says *it is not*, read it as *it is*. That will show you exactly what goes wrong in relationships. When love is not patient and love is not kind, that causes a problem. If one is envious, boastful, and self-seeking, that is not love. You can see what I mean, finish doing this with the rest of the verse. When a relationship fails, they are not following the words written in the Bible about love in this verse, and in fact about the message of love throughout the whole Bible, God is Love.

I pray for you, my grandchildren, and all young people, that you will practice these verses throughout your lives. You will not just casually read them but live what it says each and every day. I want you to have successful marriages and grow together in your faith and love together. Not only for yourselves, but also for the children that I pray you will be blessed with.

Grampy and I have not been the perfect couple, the perfect parent, or perfect grandparent, but we have always had a great love for each other. We have always and will always love each of you forever. We are not called to be perfect, only God is perfect, but we are called to love God and to strive to follow the words of the verses in 1 Corinthians 13:4-7 so we can perfectly love one another.

So, Garrett, Liam, Jordan, Jonah, and Brayden, take these words to heart and always talk to your girlfriend and your boyfriend if you are thinking about getting married. Be open and honest with each other and discuss each part of this scripture and share what it means to each of you to find if you both have the same love for each other, not just on your wedding day when you are so very much in love, but for always as man and wife when the hard times present themselves.

Yes, there have been divorces in our family. It makes me sad, but there are reasons when they are necessary. God addresses the reasons in His written Word. There are many scriptures telling when a wife or husband should not stay in a marriage, God does not want anyone to suffer in a marriage. Reading these verses, I could see that divorce was necessary within our family. Like our HeavenlyFather, I would not want anyone to remain in a marriage that has no love or where there is no respect for one another. I would not want anyone to stay in a marriage where there is physical or emotional abuse; neglect in responsibility; greed or self-seeking or other circumstances for a divorce as described in the scriptures. As sad as it can be, sometimes it is necessary. But with a love based on God's word, I do pray that you will all have a happy, love filled, successful marriage one day. That is God's wish for all married couples.

We all do and will face hard times, but we will always make it through to the other side when we live obedient to God's Word. Put Him first in your thoughts and you will always remember to make sure love is your goal in everything. If you don't allow the evil thoughts and feelings to take over, your marriage will be a lasting and wonderful one, even with the bumps along the way. Love with a pure heart, learn to laugh together and celebrate getting over the bumps together and be thankful for a lesson learned.

This is the very best I can leave for you. When I am no longer here on this earth, I will have left knowing I have done the best I knew how; helping to guide you to live in the light of

God's love. I will be rejoicing because I am assured that I will see you all again one day for eternity. That is God's promise, and I believe it.

"So, we fix our eyes not on what is seen,
but on what is unseen, since what is seen is temporary,
*but what is unseen is **eternal**."*
--2 Corinthians 4:18 (NIV)

Gary and me with our two oldest grandsons,
Garrett (Lori) and Liam (Jacob).

Jordan, Jonah (Jason and Lisa) and me.
Our third and fourth grandchildren.

Brayden (Lori) -- our fifth grandchild.

Conclusion: The Good News

"Do not conform to the pattern of this world but be transformed by the renewing of your mind. Then you will be able to test and approve what God's will is —his good, pleasing and perfect will."
--Romans 12:2 (NIV)

The more you study God's Word, the more you are less afraid of dying. We are promised a new Heaven and a new earth one day. That new earth might be this earth we live on after it is renovated and restored by God, or it may be a new planet. This is for God to decide. I do not know for sure whether it will be this earth or a new one, but we are told that it will be more beautiful and wonderful than we can ever imagine, and there will be no sickness, no death, no pain. As you study, you will see that we will be the same person, only we will be transformed, having a new, glorified body for eternity, and we will know one another. God will destroy all evil and redeem humanity, and He will dwell among us.

> *"And I heard a loud voice from the throne saying, 'Look! God's dwelling place is now among the people, and he will dwell with*

them. They will be his people, and God himself will be with them and be their God. He will wipe every tear from their eyes. There will be no more death or mourning or crying or pain, for the old order of things has passed away.'"

--Revelation 21:3-4 (NIV)

That is the Good News. Why would you not want to believe in Jesus and God and know you have so much to look forward to? It is a promise for all of us who believe in and love the Lord. This is a lot to take in and a lot to understand if you do not seek the truth in the Word. The Bible is confusing to just take bits and pieces of it and try to understand it. It is important to have help when reading and studying it, especially when you are a new believer.

This is why it is so important to listen to Bible preaching ministers and teachers. We are warned of false teaching, so make sure you know that sermons you listen to are being taught from the Bible with the Old and New Testament in it. Make sure the Bible you study contains 66 separate books compiled in it, 39 of the books are called the Old Testament and 27 books are called the New Testament. Remember, as mentioned before, *The Gospel of John*, the fourth book in the New Testament, is the best place to start when you begin studying the Word of God. You need to first believe that Jesus is the son of God and all that He did for us, and by believing, you will have life in His name for eternity.

Say a little prayer asking for understanding as you read

and get into the Word more and more. Don't beat yourself up and get discouraged if you don't understand it at first. As you read, write down what you want to know more about to help you understand and research it. Ask others about it; use study guides that are available to help make it clearer to you. Remember to choose a version of the Bible that is easy for you to read and understand. Start reading just ten or twenty minutes each day, and as you go along, you will want to read more and more. But do read some each day. If you are seeking to learn about God with all your heart, He will reveal Himself to you. God does not lie; He will keep His promise to all who believe in Him.

Here are a few more verses from God's Word that tell us of His promise to those who believe and never turn from Him:

"For God so loved the world that He gave His only begotten Son, that whoever believes in Him should not perish but have everlasting life." -- John 3:16 (NIV)

"Submit yourselves, then, to God. Resist the devil, and he will flee from you. Come near to God and he will come near to you." --James 4:7-8a (NIV)

"The Lord is not slow in keeping his promise, as some understand slowness. Instead, he is patient with you, not wanting anyone to perish, but everyone to come to repentance."
--2 Peter 3:9 (NIV)

"In keeping with His promise, we are looking forward to a new heaven and a new earth, where righteousness dwells."
--2 Peter 3:13 (NIV)

"In my Father's house are many mansions; if it were not so, I would have told you, I go to prepare a place for you. And if I go and prepare a place for you, I will come again and receive you to Myself; that where I am, there you may be also."
--John 14:2 (ESV)

Keep your eyes on the Lord; He will always be there whenever you call out to Him when you believe and trust in Him. Don't get frustrated if you fall back at times; everyone does and will. Repent and ask for forgiveness and you will be forgiven.

The great evangelist, Billy Graham, a man who truly loved the Lord and lived his life telling the world about God's love for us, even went to the Lord in prayer to confess when he felt he was not living the way he should. We all need to talk with God daily. These quotes from Billy Graham encourage me to know I am forgiven because I believe in Jesus and love the Lord and talk with Him when I am troubled, and He listens.

> *"Lord, so often I have walked on my own*
> *instead of walking in Your Spirit. Guide*
> *my footsteps this day. I pray in Jesus' name."*

> *"The Christian Life is not a constant high. I*
> *have my moments of deep discouragement. I*
> *have to go to God in prayer with tears in my*
> *eyes, and say, O God, forgive me, or help me."*

> *"How often we commit our burdens to the*
> *Lord and then fail to trust Him by taking matters*
> *into our own hands. Then, when we have messed*
> *things up, we pray, 'Oh, Lord, help me, I'm in*
> *trouble.' The choice is yours. Do you want to trust*
> *your life in God's 'pocket' or keep it in your own?"*

I choose God's pocket. My belief assures me that when I take my last breath on earth, I will take my next breath in Heaven. My prayer for all of you is that you will have that same assurance. **In JESUS' name I pray, Amen.**

Christian Artists and Songs I Enjoy

Crowder	"Lift Your Head Weary Sinner"
	"Prove It"
	"All My Hope"
	"Good God Almighty"
Zach Williams	"Chains"
	"Fear is a Liar"
	"Rescue Story"
	"Less Like Me"
Andrew Ripp	"Jericho"
King & Country	"Together"
	"God Only Knows"
	"Joy"
Toby Mac	"Help is on the Way"
	"Lose My Soul"
	"Forgiveness"
	"Me Without You"
Colton Dixon	"Miracles"
	"The Devil is a Liar"
	"Let Them See You"
	"Through All of It"
Need to Breathe	"Who Am I"
	"Brother Difference"
	"Maker Multiplies"
	"Hard Love"
Ant Clemons & Justin Timberlake	"Better Days"
Cory Asbury	"The Father's House"

	"Dear God"
	"Sparrows"
Big Daddy Weave	"This is What We Live For"
	"Redeemed!"
	"Know"
Casting Crows	"Nobody"
	"Who Am I?"
	"One Step Away"
	"Start Right Here"
	"Thrive"
	"Only Jesus"
Lauren Daigle	"You Say"
	"Still Rolling Stones"
	"Rescue"
	"Look Up Child"
	"Hold on to Me"
Snoop Dog	"Grateful"
Richlin	"Love Like Thunder"
David Dunn	"Yes & No"
Jeremy Camp	"Keep Me in the Moment"
	"Dead Man Walking"
	"The Answer"
Mercy Me	"Say I Won't"
	"Even If"
Austin French	"Wake Up Sleeper"
Cain	"Rise Up (Lazarus)"
The Afters	"Well Done"
	"I Will Fear No More"
Sanctus Real	"Confidence"
Clint Brown feat.	"Thankful"
Jason Crabb	

Stars Grow Dim	"Heaven on Earth"
Jason Crabb feat. Gary LeVox – (Rascal Flatts)	"Chose to Be My Friend"
Sidewalk Prophets	"Chosen"
	"Smile"
Tenth Avenue North	"Control (Somehow You Want Me)"
Francesca Battistelli	"The Breakup Song"
	"Defender"
Brandon Lake (Elevation Worship)	"Graves to Garden"
	"Faith Hope Love Repeat"
Matt Maher	"Lord, I Need You"
	"What a Friend"
	"Your Love Defends Me"

Works Cited

Becker, Joshua. "Martin Buxbaum on Success."
    becomingminimalist. 2021.

Copeland, Kenneth. "From Faith to Faith: Daily Devotional - 'Real
    Intercession.'" September 2022. www.kcm.org.

JMM Team. Josh McDowell Ministry. "Crucifixion Details of
    the Resurrection of Christ: Apologetics Booklet Examines
    Factual Evidence of the Death and Rise of Jesus Christ."
    March 2017. www.JoshMcDowellMinistry.com

McNamara, H.C., S.C. Kane, J.M. Craig, R.V. Short, M.P.
    Umstead. "A Review of the Mechanisms and Evidence
    for Typical and Atypical Twinning." American Journal
    of Obstetrics and Gynecology. February 2016. 214 (2).
    2015. 10. 930. PMID 26548710. pp. 172-191.
    https://1016/j. ajog.doi.org/.

Pape, O., N. Winer, A. Paumier, H. J. Philippe, B. Flatrès, G.
    Boog. "Superfetation: About a Case and Review of the
    Literature." EM Consulte Journal Obstetrics and
    Reproductive Biology.

Yvette Smith Kilgore's Biography

Yvette lives in Myrtle Beach, South Carolina, after previously living in Ohio, Turkey, California, and North Carolina. She and her husband, Gary, enjoy traveling and most of all, love being with their family.

They are proud parents of one daughter, two sons, and five grandchildren. All are loved "A bushel and a peck and a hug around the neck," as she tells them every chance she can, with a hug around the neck included.

Yvette felt inspired to share experiences from her past to tell others about the love of God with the hope it will help others to know of God's goodness and mercy.

She and Gary share their home and their bed with their miniature golden doodle, Eddie.

Eddie, me, and Gary.

Additional Books Available At Here I Am Publishing, LLC

Richard's Key

Roy's Sandman

A Stranger to Myself

The Clumsy Little Angel

Three Day Nights

All for Him

Silent Victims (Devotional)

Hands Reaching, Hearts Touching (Devotional)

You Can't Kill the Miracle

The Good Sheriff

God's Hands

A Melody that Can't Be Forgotten

Coming Soon from
Here I Am Publishing, LLC

Above the Overpass by Linda Stapleton

Firefly Forest by Tom W. Winslow

Camden and His Superpower Ears by Leigh Cutrone

The Art of Law by Tom W. Winslow

Tragedy, Survival, Triumph by Bill Duckworth

The Lantern by Kathleen Pedersen

Kilgore Clan

CPSIA information can be obtained
at www.ICGtesting.com
Printed in the USA
LVHW082039031222
734536LV00016B/762